Hrotsvit of Gandersheim:
A Florilegium of her Works

Library of Medieval Women

ISSN 1369–9652

Series Editor: Jane Chance

Already published

Christine de Pizan's Letter of Othea to Hector, *Jane Chance*, 1990

The Writings of Margaret of Oingt, Medieval Prioress and Mystic, *Renate Blumenfeld-Kosinski*, 1990

Saint Bride and her Book: Birgitta of Sweden's Revelations, *Julia Bolton Holloway*, 1992

The Memoirs of Helene Kottanner (1439–1440), *Maya Bijvoet Williamson*, 1998

The Writings of Teresa de Cartagena, *Dayle Seidenspinner-Núñez*, 1998

Julian of Norwich: *Revelations of Divine Love* and *The Motherhood of God*: an excerpt, *Frances Beer*, 1998

Hildegard of Bingen: On Natural Philosophy and Medicine: Selections from *Cause et cure, Margret Berger*, 1999

Women Saints' Lives in Old English Prose, *Leslie A. Donovan*, 1999

Angela of Foligno's *Memorial, Cristina Mazzoni (trans. John Cirignano)*, 1999

Hrotsvit of Gandersheim:
A Florilegium of her Works

Translated with Introduction, Interpretative Essay and Notes

Katharina M. Wilson
University of Georgia

D. S. BREWER

First published 1998
D. S. Brewer, Cambridge
Reprinted 2000

ISBN 0 85991 489 5

D. S. Brewer is an imprint of Boydell and Brewer Ltd
PO Box 9, Woodbridge, Suffolk IP12 3DF, UK
and of Boydell and Brewer Inc.
PO Box 41026, Rochester, NY 14604–4126, USA

A catalogue record for this book is available
from the British Library

Library of Congress Cataloging-in-Publication Data
Hrotsvitha, ca. 935–ca. 975.
    [Selections. English]
    Hrotsvit of Gandersheim : a florilegium of her works / translated
with introduction, interpretative essay and notes, Katharina Wilson.
        p.   cm. – (Library of medieval women, ISSN 1369–9652)
    Includes bibliographical references and index.
    ISBN 0–85991–489–5 (paperback : alk. paper)
    1. Hrotsvitha, ca. 935–ca. 975 – Translations into English.
2. Christian literature, Latin (Medieval and modern) – Translations
into English.   3. Christian drama, Latin (Medieval and modern) –
Translations into English.   4. Epic poetry, Latin (Medieval and
modern) – Translations into English.   5. Women and literature –
Germany – Saxony – History.   6. Christian saints – Legends.
I. Wilson, Katharina M.   II. Title.   III. Series.
PA8340.A28   1998
872'.03–dc21   97–51129

This publication is printed on acid-free paper

Printed in Great Britain by
Athenæum Press Ltd, Gateshead, Tyne & Wear

Contents

Introduction

L ong considered the "rara avis" of early Germanic authors, Hrotsvit of Gandersheim has now been firmly placed in the medieval monastic traditions of Benedictine spirituality, and even though her hagiographic plays are without precedent in tenth century European literature, her efforts at the didactic utilization of hagiography are not. In fact, Hrotsvit's dramatization of legendary materials bears testimony to the prominent role that hagiographic *lectiones* played in the Benedictine office and to the gradual rise of the use of hagiographic *exempla* in homiletic texts. While illustrative *exempla* were copied and circulated throughout the Middle Ages, the actual logical organization of homiletic narratives – whereby individual *exempla* became linked with dogmatic or scriptural topics – did not occur until the rise of the preaching orders. As early as the twelfth century, several *exempla* collections, alphabetically arranged and painstakingly cross-referenced, were available for preachers – the best known, perhaps, being Etienne de Bourbon's *Liber de septem donis*. Hrotsvit's thematic linkage of her plays to the liturgy and her utilization of hagiographic sources in a plethora of non-hagiographic genres are, thus, while early and imaginative, yet by no means totally alien to the early medieval literary scene famous for its predilection for genre mixing. To argue against the authenticity of her works on these grounds does not, therefore, seem to be tenable.

Manuscripts

The most complete text of Hrotsvit's works is preserved in the Emmeram-Munich Codex (clm 14485 1–150). This is also the oldest extant copy of her works dating to the early eleventh century. The manuscript, believed to have been produced at Gandersheim, was discovered by the leading German humanist Conrad Celtis in 1494 and was printed under the auspices of the Sodalitas Rhenana by Hieronymus Holtzel in Nuremberg in 1501. The first edition contains six woodcuts illustrating the dramas: two by Albrecht Dürer and four believed to be by Wolfgang Traut. Celtis made emendations to the text but Johannes Tritheim commissioned a complete copy of the manuscript prior to Celtis' editing. This original version is preserved in the Schlossbibliothek of Pommersfelden (cod. 308 (2883)). Additionally, several fragmentary texts of Hrotsvit's works have been discovered in the twentieth century. Goswin Frenken found a copy of the first four dramas (perhaps the copy Hrotsvit claims to have sent to certain *sapientes* for evaluation). They are preserved in a manuscript of miscellaneous texts in the Cologne Stadtarchiv (cod. w 101, 1–16) and were copied toward the end of the twelfth century, probably from a prototype other than the Emmeram-Munich codex. Another late twelfth century copy of *Gallicanus* was incorporated into the *Alderspach Passionale* (clm 2552, now in Munich) and, as some scholars have argued, in the late twelfth century and early thirteenth century from here into the *Magnum Legendarium Austriacum* without attribution of authorship (Heiligenkreuz Stiftsbibliothek, cod. 12, vol. 278–81; Österreichische Nationalbibliothek, Vienna, cod. lat. 336, vol. 362–66; Melk Stiftsbibliothek, cod. 675, vol. 234–38).[1]

Biography

All we know of Hrotsvit's biography has to be gleaned from her dedicatory letters and prefaces. She was probably born in the fourth decade of the tenth century, and is likely to have been of noble Saxon descent. She lived as a canoness in the Imperial Abbey of Gandersheim under Gerberga II's rule, and she probably died at the turn of the millennium after having completed her last extant work, the *Primordia*, in 973.[2]

Living in the tenth century Benedictine monastic environment, Hrotsvit's predilection for choosing hagiographic sources that celebrate the hermetical and monastic ideal of *soli-deo vivere* comes as no surprise. It is evident from her work that she considers hermetic life (total solitude in worship) and martyrdom as the two most privileged manifestations of Christian devotion. In eremitic life, as H. Fichtenau observes, "... separation [from the world] was stressed almost to the point of pathos."[3] In an age where temporary solitude (in taking one's meals, spending one's day) was a most serious monastic punishment, eremitism and martyrdom do, indeed, appear to be metaphorical equivalents of self-denial. Two of her plays, *Paphnutius* and *Abraham* particularly, reflect a specifically German brand of monastic hermetism, the custom of "Klausner" and "Klausner-

---

1   The most complete editions of Hrotsvit's works are still those of Paul von Winterfeld, *Hrotsvithae Opera* (Berlin: Weidmann, 1965) and Helena Homeyer, *Hrotsvithae Opera* (Munich: Schoninge, 1970). For a full discussion of the manuscript tradition see Sibylle Jefferies, "Hrotsvit and the *Magnum Legendarium Austriacum*," in *Hrotsvit of Gandersheim, "Rara avis in Saxonia"*, ed. K. Wilson, Medieval and Renaissance Monograph Series, vol. VII (Ann Arbor, 1987), pp. 239–52.

2   She says in the *Primordia* (525) that she was born "longo tempore" after the death of Otto of Saxony (died November 30, 912) and that she was older than her Abbess Gerberga (born c.940).

3   Heinrich Fichtenau, *Living in the Tenth Century*, trans. P. Geary (Chicago: University of Chicago Press, 1991), p. 246.

innen" (*inclusi* and *inclusae*), a practice whereby religious people did not live in a monastery but, rather, next to a convent or church in individual claustration, walled up in a cell without doors. Martyrdom, conversely, is celebrated in two of her dramas (*Dulcitius* and *Sapientia*) and three of her legends (*Pelagius, Dionysius,* and *Agnes*); in all but one of the five treatments of martyrdom the saint dies not only as an eloquent witness to the faith but in preserving her/his virginity from persuasive assaults by male antagonists. Both (hermetism and martyrdom) are extreme, even extremist forms of asceticism depicted by Hrotsvit not simply as idealized abstractions of Christological emulation but as manifestations of the eternal human struggle for moral excellence.

In composing all her texts Hrotsvit is entirely within the mainstream of the didactic hagiographic *exemplum*'s tradition which invariably presented action in the texts as particular and anecdotal. By extension, her treatment of sin and virtue is never abstract but exemplified by specific instances of good and evil behavior and always anchored in a recognizable historic, geographic, and social context, inevitably constructed rhetorically with an eye to its closure conveying its moral.

Hrotsvit's epics exhibit the same concerns for particular detail and moral intention. Her conception of history in general, and of Otto's *imperium* in specific, was more complex and sophisticated than those of Benedict of Saint Andrea and Thietmar of Merseburg, in that she recognized that Otto's imperial title and dignity absorbed his royalty. She knew, as Carl Erdmann has argued, ". . . that Otto's empire had universal preeminence . . . [and she] . . . conferred upon Otto the Caesarian and Augustan *imperium* and placed him in the same line of succession with the ancient emperors."[4] As such, she is able to anchor his deeds not only in hagiography (by depicting him as the true imperial *christomimētēs*) but also in the lore of ancient Roman grandeur.

Even Hrotsvit's name has been the source of some discussion.[5] She records the nominative form of her name as Hrotsvit (in the "Epistle" [3] and in the prologue [1] to the third book) and the inflected forms as being Hrotsvithae ("Maria" [18], "Ascensio" [148], "Gongolf" [3]) and Hrotsvitham ("Pelagius" [3]). After many fanciful interpretations of her name, ranging from Gottsched's "Weisse Rose" to "Rauschewind" and "rascher Witz,"[6] it was not until 1838 that Jacob Grimm in *Lateini-*

---

4 Karl Erdmann, "Das ottonische Reich als Imperium Romanum," in *Deutsches Archiv für Geschichte des Mittelalters* VI (1943): 422.

5 The following page is a summary of my note "Clamor Validus Gandershemensis," *Germanic Notes* 14, no. 2 (1983): 17–18.

6 Edwin Zeydel, " 'Ego Clamor Validus' – Hrotsvitha," *Modern Language Notes* 64 (1946): 282.

sche Gedichte des 10. und 11. Jahrhunderts recognized that Hrotsvit herself gave us the Latin etymology of her name.[7] She says in the prose introduction to the dramas (3): "Unde ego, Clamor Validus Gandeshemensis non recusavi illum imitari dictando dum alii colunt legendo." Grimm pointed out that her old Saxon name derived from the two words hruot = clamor = voice and suid = validus = strong. As she wrote "Clamor Validus Gandeshemensis" in apposition to "ego", he observed she must have intended it either as a mere Latinization of her name or as a pun. No one before Grimm, not even the German Humanists who so enthusiastically furthered her literary fortunes, has the "faintest inkling of the true derivation" of Hrotsvit's name.[8] In the seventeenth century, Martin F. Seidel even went so far as to consider "Hrotsvit" to be an anagram for Helena von Rossow and claimed, accordingly, that Hrotsvit was a member of the Brandenburg von Rossow family.[9]

"Clamor Validus," however, is both an interpretation of, and a pun on, Hrotsvit's name – one that she chose to represent her poetic program as well as her poetic purpose.[10] It is not merely a Latinization of "Hrotsvit" but, more important, an interpretation of it and an explanation of her self and of her earthly mission as suggested by her name. Seen as allegorization of her name, "Clamor Validus" could be best rendered as "Forceful Testimony" (that is, for God), or "Vigorous (valid) Attestation" (that is of Christian truth).[11]

Nothing is known of Hrotsvit's childhood and ancestry except that she was of noble Saxon parentage. With pride in her descent from the famous

---

7   Jacob Grimm, *Lateinische Gedichte des 10. und 11. Jahrhunderts* (Göttingen: Dieterische Buchhandlung, 1898) p. 9.

8   Zeydel, "Ego Clamor Validus," p. 282.

9   *Ibid.*

10   *Ibid.* Grimm's contribution to Hrotsvit scholarship rests with his recognition of the connection between her name and the reference to herself as "Clamor Validus." His conclusion, on the other hand, has subsequently been modified. Sebastian Euringer, for example, asserts: "Denn ihr Name bedeutet eigentlich nicht 'mächtiger Ruf,' sondern 'am Ruhm Mächtig,' " and he adds: "Ich wenigstens finde für *hruot* nur *fama, gloria*, nirgends aber *clamor* angegeben, was althochdeutsch *hruop* heissen würde" ("Drei Beiträge zur Roswotha Forschung," *Historisches Jahrbuch der Goerres-Gesellschaft zur Pflege des Wissenshaft im katholischen Deutschland* 54 (1934): 75–83). Thus, when Hrotsvit identifies herself as "ego Clamor Validus" rather than as "Fama (Gloria) Valida," she must have had in mind reasons other than the mere Latinization of her name.

11   Euringer "Drei Beiträge," p. 76, suggests that "Clamor Validus" is a reference to John the Baptist ("ego vox clamantis in deserto: Dirigete viam Domini!" (John 1:24)), with whose mission and zeal Hrotsvit identified herself and who appeared to Oda, the foundress of Gandersheim, in a vision. Interpreting the meaning of her name in this way, Hrotsvit stands in the mainstrean of early medieval thought, which insisted that *sine nomine persona non est* and that every word, every name, like everything, had a transcendental meaning and reflected the divine plan of the Creator.

tribe of the warlike Saxons, Hrotsvit gives us the etymology of the name of her tribe (*gens Saxonum*) in the *Gesta* (4–5):

Ad claram gentem Saxonum nomen habentem
A Saxon per duritiam mentis bene firmam.

That she was of noble descent is almost certain, since only daughters of the aristocracy were admitted to Gandersheim, a foundation of the Liudolf dynasty in lower Saxony on the slopes of the Harz mountains, on the border between the dioceses of Hildesheim and Mainz.[12] In 852, thirty years after the first Saxon foundation at Herford, Gandersheim Abbey was established by Liudolf and his wife, Oda, ancestors of the Ottos. Initially the canonesses dwelt at Brunschausen and were moved only four years later to Gandersheim. Five of Liudolf's daughters took the veil, and three of them become the first abbesses of Gandersheim. Hathumonda (852–74), educated at Herford, Gerberta I (874–96), and Christina (896–918) ruled for twenty-two years, and they succeeded not only in enforcing religious discipline but also in making the abbey into a new center of learning. The Liudolfs maintained close ties with their foundations: Liudolf himself was lay abbot of Brunschausen, his son Otto was lay abbot of Hersfeld,[13] and Oda retired to Gandersheim Abbey after her husband's death. Agius of Corvey, brother of the three Liudolf abbesses, gives testimony to the spirit of learning and culture in the abbey in the erudite dialogue of solace which he composed for the canonesses after Hathumonda's death.

The Liudolf dynasty showed a predilection for establishing religious houses, especially for daughters of the aristocracy. That some of these convents and abbeys became centers of learning and culture is hardly surprising, given the illustrious history of female monasticism. "Monasteries for women," as Suzanne Wemple observes, "were centers of civilization and culture in the early Middle Ages."[14] Some scriptoria of Frankish and Merovingian convents were the workplaces of nuns, Cologne and Chelles being the most famous. Bernhard Bischoff, for example, has connected with these scriptoria seventeen codices that contain the names of several female scribes.[15] Indeed, "some of the best examples of calligraphy," Florence E. de Roover remarks, "came from the hands

---

12 See, for example, Wilhelm Gundlach, *Heldenlieder der deutschen Kaiserzeit* (Aalen: Scientia, 1970), pp. 225ff; Duckett, *Death and Life*, pp. 182ff.

13 Mariane Schütze-Plugk, *Herrscher und Märtyrerauffassung bei Hrotsvit von Gandersheim* (Wiesbaden: Steiner, 1972), p. 5.

14 Suzanne F. Wemple, *Women in Frankish Society* (Philadelphia: University of Pennsylvania Press, 1981), p. 175.

15 Bernard Bischoff, "Die Kölner Nonnenhandschriften und das Skriptorium von Chelles," in *Mittelalterliche Studien*, ed. Bischoff (Stuttgart: Hiersemann, 1966), pp. 16–33.

of nuns." Some of these scribes, she points out, were also very prolific: Dietmundis (c.1060–1130) of Wessobrunn, Bavaria, for instance, left a catalogue of forty-five volumes that she herself had copied,[16] and religious women made lasting contributions in the fields of hagiography and hymnography as well.[17]

By the tenth century Gandersheim, like Reichenau, Tegernsee, Saint Gall, Fulda, Corvey, Herford, and Saint Emmeram (with the last four Gandersheim Abbey entertained close connections), was an oasis of intellectual and spiritual activity. Like the other great medieval monasteries, it functioned as a school, hospital, library, political center, house of refuge, center of pilgrimage. As such, it harbored different kinds of people, one of whom might have been the Spaniard who claimed to have been an eyewitness to Pelagius's martyrdom and told Hrotsvit the story of the martyrdom of the new saint in Cordoba.[18] Incidentally, the Emmeram-Munich codex of Hrotsvit's works also contains on the back of the last page eight lines in the old Glagolitic alphabet. They are almost certainly not by Hrotsvit, but they help to date the codex and give testimony to the cosmopolitan atmosphere that prevailed in Gandersheim during the Ottonian Renaissance. The old Glagolitic alphabet was used in Bulgaria and Croatia in the tenth century; perhaps Hrotsvit's abbey or Saint Emmeram harbored someone from the Balkans,[19] or the codex may even have traveled to the Balkans.

Gandersheim was a free abbey directly responsible to the king rather than to the Church. Indeed, in 947 Otto I freed the abbey from royal rule and gave the abbess the authority to have her own court of law, keep her own army, coin her own money, and hold a seat in the Imperial Diet. In 918 the reign of the three Liudolf abbesses was followed by the interregnum of two women not affiliated with the crown but chosen by the sisters from among themselves. The first of these abbesses was Hrotsvit I, whose name Hrotsvit might have been chosen or to whom she may have been related. In 965 the rule of a royal abbess was reinstated with the conse-

---

16 Florence E. de Roover, "The Scriptorium," in *The Medieval Library*, ed. James W. Thompson (Chicago: University of Chicago Press, 1939), pp. 609, 610.

17 Wemple, *Women in Frankish Society*, p. 181. Wemple observes, "While Merovingian legal texts were the products of episcopal and royal courts, saints' lives, hymns, and prayers were closely connected with the monasteries. Nuns left an imprint on this type of literature by introducing feminine ideals into hagiography and leaving a record of their own mystical experiences." Baudovinia's "Life of Saint Radegund," Aldegund's *vita* recording her visions, Hugeburc's "Life of Saint Wynnebald," and the older version from Chelles, of Saint Balthild's *vita* bear eloquent testimony to this observation.

18 Nagel, *Hrotsvit von Gandersheim*, Stuttgart, Metzlersche Verlagsbuchhandlung, 1965, p. 47; Homeyer, *Hrotsvithae Opera*, p. 124.

19 Edwin Zeydel, "On the Two Minor Poems in the Hrotsvitha Codex," *Modern Language Notes* 60 (1945): 376.

cration of Gerberga II (940–1001), daughter of Henry of Bavaria and niece of Otto I, by Bishop Otwin of Hildesheim. During the reign of Abbess Gerberga II, Gandersheim was renowned for its scholastic, cultural, and religious activities.[20]

The date of Hrotsvit's entrance into Gandersheim is uncertain, but given the traditions of the time, it is likely that she was quite young.[21] She lived, studied, and wrote during the abbey's golden age under Gerberga II's rule, a period of peace, tranquillity, and genuine devotion to learning and service. Hrotsvit's virtuosity in adorning her works with diverse rhetorical ornaments (she uses, as I have argued elsewhere, almost all of the figures and tropes discussed by Donatus, Isidore, and the Venerable Bede), as well as the *etymologia, arithmetica*, and *musica* lessons incorporated into her plays, bear eloquent testimony to her training in, and respect for, the *artes*. According to her own statement in the preface to the legends, her teachers were Rikkardis and Gerberga II. It seems that Rikkardis, whom Hrotsvit describes as being "sapientissima atque benignissima magistra," taught her the curriculum of the quadrivium, while Gerberga perfected her in the fields of the trivium. Gerberga herself was educated in Saint Emmeram, the cultural center of Bavaria. It was she who introduced Hrotsvit to the Roman authors as well as to the patristic writers. Like her sister, Hadwig of Swabia, who was known for her connections with Ekkehard II of Saint Gall, Gerberga seems also to have received tuition in Greek;[22] indeed, her knowledge of Greek, as Bert Nagel

---

20 This is reflected by one of the letters of Otto II to Gerberga in which, sending his five-year-old daughter Sophia to be educated in the abbey, the emperor praised the cultural state of the abbey:

> Nos dilectae conjugis nostrae Theophanae
> Imperatricis Augustae votum et interventionem
> Sequentes filiam nostram carissimam nomine Sopiam
> Deo sanctaeque Genitrici illius Mariae virgini
> Sanctisque confessoribus Anastasio et Innocentio,
> Quorum Ecclesia in loco Gandesheim nominato
> Honorifice constructa videtur, cui etiam Gerbig
> Neptis nostra sub praesenti tempore venerabilis
> Abbatissa praesse dignoscitur devoto animo obtulimus
> Atque sacrae scripturae litteras ut ibi ediscat
> vitamque et conversationem dignam Sanctimonialium Deo
> Ibi servientium imitetur.

21 The first abbesses of Gandersheim entered their monasteries at a young age. Hathumonda, for example, entered Herford at the age of six, and Sophia, Otto II's and Theophano's daughter, was sent to Gandersheim for education at the age of five. However, the suggestion, first voiced by Magnin in his edition of Hrotsvit's works, that Hrotsvit shows such deep understanding of erotic passion that she must have taken the veil rather late in life, enjoyed for a while at least some popularity with German Hrotsvit scholars.

22 Wilhelm Gundlach in *Heldenlieder der deutschen Kaiserzeit* (Aalen: Scientia, 1970), vol. I, pp. 26ff, tells that Hadwig spoke and translated Greek. She learned the language while she

suggests, might have been an additional reason why Otto II's Byzantine wife, Theophano, spent much time in Gandersheim.[23] In addition, as Peter Dronke suggests, Hrotsvit may have received some instruction at court:

> It is possible that she spent some of her youth at the Ottonian court rather than in a convent. One detail here seems to me particularly suggestive. In 952 Otto I had invited Rather, the most widely-read scholar and most brilliant prose-writer of the age, to his court. . . . Ostensibly he came to give Bruno some advanced literary teaching; but the fact that Rather cultivated a distinctive style of rhymed prose, which has notable parallels in Hrotsvitha, makes it tempting to suppose that, in Rather's years with Otto, Hrotsvitha too received instruction from him, and then tried to model some of her mannerisms on his. Especially her longest and most complicated sentences . . . have to me a markedly Ratherian ring.[24]

It was through Theophano that the great culture of Byzantium came directly to Saxony. In addition to transmitting Greek arts and customs, Theophano also introduced many refinements from the court of Constantinople, such as wearing silks and taking baths.[25] She may have been, as Franz Dölger argues, an important factor in the new conception of Imperial majesty at the Saxon court.[26] Significantly, perhaps, for Hrotsvit's dramatic ventures, the Greek princess was related to Constantine VII, author of the *Liber de ceremoniis*. Constantine mentions, among other ceremonial concerns, the substitution of religious pageants for pagan spectacles. Liudprand of Cremona, too, observes that an embryonic church drama existed in tenth century Byzantium. Sent by Otto I as his ambassador to the Emperor Nichephoras Phocas in order to arrange the marriage of Otto II and a Greek princess, Liudprand complained in his work *Mission to Constantinople* that Hagia Sophia was turned into a theater, and he recorded a scenic depiction of the ascension of the prophet Elias.[27]

was engaged to the Greek King Constantino. As a widow, she read Virgil together with Ekkehard II of Saint Gall. In addition, as Nagel (*Hrotsvit von Gandersheim*, p. 43) remarks, the document of Pope John XIII for the abbey records Gerberga's name in Greek letters.

23 Bodo of Clus records that Theophano frequently visited Gandersheim Abbey on holy days. See also Nagel, *Hrotsvit von Gandersheim*, p. 43.

24 Peter Dronke, *Women Writers of the Middle Ages: A Critical Study of Texts from Perpetua († 203) to Marguerite Porete († 1310)* (Cambridge: Cambridge University Press, 1984), pp. 5, 6.

25 Anne Lyon Haight, *Hrotswitha of Gandersheim: Her Life, Ties, and Works and a Comprehensive Bibliography* (New York: Hrotswitha Club, 1965), p. 9.

26 Franz Dögler, "Die Ottonenkaiser und Byzanz," in *Karolingische und Ottonische Kunst*, ed. H. Subin *et al.* (Wiesbaden: Frans Steiner, 1957).

27 Cf. Rudolf Vey, *Christliches Theater im Mittelalter und Neuzeit* (Aschaffenburg: P. Pattlock, 1960), p. 12.

In addition to visiting Gandersheim frequently, Theophano also sent her daughter Sophia there to be educated. Otto II, soon after his coronation in 973, bequeathed his Seesen property to the abbey, and in 975 he solemnly reaffirmed all previous gifts to Gandersheim.[28] Hrotsvit thus was directly exposed to contact with the Imperial family, which was profoundly Byzantine in its cultural outlook and personal tastes. Perhaps as a result, a large portion of her sources belong to the hagiography of the Byzantine Empire. Four of her legends (*Maria, Ascensio, Theophilius, Basilius*) and four of her dramas (*Calimachus, Abraham, Paphnutius, Sapientia*) have their roots in the hagiography of the Eastern Church. It may be conjectured that Hrotsvit's contact with the Imperial family and its orientation to Byzantine culture and tastes might have been a contributing factor in her interest in Eastern sources.

Works

Hrotsvit's works consist of eight legends, six plays, two epics, and a short poem. The works are organized chronologically and generically into three books and fall into three clearly marked creative periods, the breaks occurring after the fourth legend and the fourth play.[29]

Book I, containing the legends (seven in leonine hexameters; one, *Gongolf*, in elegiac distichs), begins with a preface and a dedication to Hrotsvit's abbess, Gerberga II. The first legend, *Maria*, is a treatment of the Virgin's life based on an apocryphal source, the *Pseudo-Evangelium* of Mattheus. In the exordium to the poem, Hrotsvit introduces her major theme: the exaltation of the virtue of steadfast, obedient, and, therefore, triumphant and life-giving virginity. *Maria* narrates the miraculous conception and birth of Mary, her childhood, and her stay at the temple, her reluctance to marry, the selection by divine judgment of Joseph as her husband, and finally, her motherhood. Mary's glorification is entirely Christocentric – her laudable chastity and exemplary conduct are subordinated to her role as genetrix, and the poem closes with a prayer to Christ. Hrotsvit's second legend, *Ascensio*, the shortest of her works, is drawn from a Greek source describing the ascension of Christ. The third legend deals with the eighth century Frankish knight Gongolf, who lived under Pippin the Short. Gongolf is the meek, courteous, wise, and chaste knight. His magnanimity and virtue, however, became the source of envy for the devil, who uses his favorite weapon, human sexuality, to plot the saintly Gongolf's destruction. Gongolf's wife, crazed with lust for a cleric, not

---

[28] Nagel, *Hrotsvit von Gandersheim*, p. 46.
[29] The following description summarizes my description of her works in *Medieval Women Writers*, ed. K.M. Wilson (Athens, University of Georgia Press, 1984), pp. 42–57.

only commits adultery but also instigates her husband's murder. Subsequently, she suffers for the deed (and her lack of contrition) by means of a scatological miracle when her blasphemy of Gongolf's miracles is punished by an involuntary fart whenever she opens her mouth. Hrotsvit's fourth legend is based not on a written source but on an eyewitness report. It describes the martyrdom of the chaste Pelagius, a tenth century Spanish saint who died persevering against the homoerotic advances of the Caliph of Cordoba, Abderrahman III. The fifth and sixth legends are the first literary treatments of the Faust theme in Germany and deal with the Greek saints Basilius and Theophilus; both concern men who made a pact with the devil and sold their immortal souls for mortal gain. The sinners are saved at the intercession of Bishop Basilius and the Virgin Mary respectively. In both poems Hrotsvit uses the themes of fall and conversion, sin and salvation; in both she apotheosizes the unlimited power of prayer and contrition that are rewarded by divine forgiveness. The seventh legend describes the martyrdom of Dionysius, the first bishop of Paris. The canoness's last legend glorifies Saint Agnes, martyr for virginity, who rejects the marriage proposal of Sempronius's son in favor of the heavenly bridegroom and resists, with Christ's help, the ignominious attempts of her adversaries to defile her chastity when she is placed in a brothel for punishment. At the conclusion of her earthly sufferings, Christ awaits his virginal bride in the celestial bridal chamber.

The second book, Hrotsvit's most widely known creation, contains her plays, all in rhymed, rhythmic prose. The book is introduced by a dedication to Gerberga, followed by a prose letter to the learned patrons of the book (sometimes identified as Gerberga's former teachers at Saint Emmeram). *Gallicanus*, the first of Hrotsvit's dramas, disseminated in the Middle Ages in martyrologies under the feast days of Saints John and Paul, deals with the conversion and martyrdom of the pagan Roman general Gallicanus. He has been promised the hand of Constantia, Emperor Constantine's daughter, if he wages a successful war against the Scythians. Constantia, however, has taken the vow of chastity, and, therefore, cannot marry him. Through divine intervention and the assistance of Saints Paul and John, Gallicanus becomes a Christian and renounces marriage. Like Constantia, he devotes the rest of his life to religion and dies persevering in his faith. *Dulcitius*, the second play, takes place during the Diocletian persecutions of the Christians and dramatizes the martyrdom of three virgin sisters, Agape, Chionia, and Hirena, who refuse to forego their faith and their chastity (thereby avoiding idolatry and adultery against the heavenly bridegroom). *Dulcitius* contains elements of an almost mimelike character. Dulcitius is depicted as a philandering pagan. He imprisons the girls in a room adjacent to the pantry so that he may visit them undisturbed at night. The girls, very much afraid, spend the hours in prayer. Dulcitius arrives at nightfall, but when he tries to seduce the virgins, a miracle happens; he is deluded and mistakes the pots and pans for the sisters. He embraces and kisses the kitchen utensils until he emerges so smeared and blackened with soot that his soldiers mistake him for the devil and the guards chase him from the palace doorsteps. This instance of typical medieval kitchen humor is an excellent example of the concretization and visualization of Hrotsvit's hagiographic themes; external appearance is a reflection of the internal state. Dulcitius, whose soul is possessed by the devil, appears as the *imago diaboli* in body.

The third play, *Calimachus*, depicts the sin and subsequent conversion of a pagan youth. Calimachus is passionately in love with Drusiana, Andronicus's wife, who has taken the vow of chastity. Upon learning of his violent passion, Drusiana prays for death in order to forego temptation, and she dies. Ablaze with lust, Calimachus bribes Fortunatus, the tomb guard, in a desperate attempt at necrophilia. Before he can profane Drusiana's body, however, he and Fortunatus both die. They are subsequently resurrected by Saint John, and Calimachus is converted to Christianity. As did Sempronius's son in *Agnes*, so Calimachus vividly exemplifies the Christian paradox that in order to live the Christian has to die to the world first.

In the fourth and fifth dramas, *Paphnutius* and *Abraham*, Hrotsvit again treats of the themes of fall and conversion. Two harlots, representing the most abominable vice of *luxuria carnis*, are converted by two saintly anchorites and consequently live ascetic lives. In *Paphnutius* the courtesan Thais is converted by a saintly hermit who aspires to this task as the result of a vision, while in *Abraham* the hermit is the courtesan's uncle and former guardian. The recognition scene between the aged Abraham, posing as a lover, and his niece Mary in the brothel has evoked especial praise for Hrotsvit's talent as a dramatist. Finally, *Sapientia*, the last of the dramas, deals with the martyrdom of the three allegorical virgins, Fides, Spes, and Karitas, who, like the heroines of *Dulcitius*, willingly face death on earth so that they may earn eternal life in heaven.

Paphnutius and *Sapientia* commence with a dialogue lesson in music and mathematics respectively. In *Paphnutius* the saintly hermit is expounding upon the mysteries of the celestial harmonies to his disciples, while in *Sapientia* the mother of the three virgins confounds the pagan emperor with her arithmetical learning or, rather, her Boethian exposition of numerical values. Book two concludes with a poem of thirty-four hexameters on Saint John's Apocalypse which is believed to have been intended for inscription under the twelve murals of Gandersheim.

Book three contains the two extant leonine hexameter epics, the

Carmen de Gestis Oddonis Imperatoris or, in short, the *Gesta* and the *Primordia Coenobii Gandeshemensis*. The *Gesta*, it has been argued, is one of the most successful tenth century attempts at a Christian epic. Otto the Great is depicted as the ideal Christian ruler – a descendant, not necessarily of Aeneas, but of David. Otto's heroic excellence, as Dennis Kratz argues, comprises characteristics derivative of the *figura* David: *sapientia, pietas, clementia, fortitudo*.[30] He is the earthly replica of the heavenly king, deriving his just power from God. By implication, insurrection against him (and there were more than a few during Hrotsvit's lifetime) is depicted as the work of the devil. Among the female characters of the *Gesta*, Otto's queens Edith and Adelheid stand out; both are depicted as paragons of feminine excellence, described in the superlatives of the hagiographic tradition and in the consciously court-oriented schemata of values.

Finally, the short *Primordia* presents the history of Gandersheim Abbey from its founding until the death of Abbess Christina in 918. The *Primordia* is replete with hagiographic topoi, legendary characters (whose exemplary lives are reminiscent of the heroes and heroines of Hrotsvit's legends and dramas), miracles, and visions. At the same time, the work also manifests a strong political tendency: any part that the Hildesheim bishops played in the foundation of the abbey is conspicuously ignored. Rather, emphasis is placed on the role of the Liudolfs in establishing an autonomous religious house that is to be entirely independent of the jurisdiction and influence of the Hildesheim bishops.

The organization of the three books in this manner shows Hrotsvit to be a master of symmetry and balance. The themes and motifs of the first book are repeated in a different generic form in the second, and there is also a statistical inversion of the predominant sex in the two books: in the legends men predominate; in the dramas women do. The hagiographic themes of the legends and dramas are transferred to a historic context in the third book. In all works the virtuous act serves as a mimetic paradigm of sanctity; Christological analogues are presented in the monastic, as well as the secular contexts.

Hrotsvit's predilection for viewing her act of creating as ordering, patterning, and arranging the details of her sources for the individual work is reflected in her prefatory texts where she refers to her act of writing as "ordinari."[31] It also holds true in terms of the arrangement of

---

30 Dennis Kratz, "The Nun's Epic: Hrotswitha on Christian Heroism," in *Wege der Worte*, ed. Donald C. Riechel (Cologne, Vienna, 1978), pp. 132–42.

31 For a detailed discussion of her prologues, see K. Wilson, *Hrotsvit of Gandersheim: Ethics of Authorial Stance* (Leyden: Brill, 1988).

the Gesamtwerk. Indeed, one pronounced particularity of the Hrotsvithean texts is the omnipresent evidence of her fondness for linkage, for ordering in a patterned, harmonious way and imbuing, in turn, the structural composition of her works with numeric symbolism that reinforces her themes. Poetologically, this patterning is the manifestation of the same creative process as that which she described in the prefaces denoting the composition of the texts; it is also analogous to her description of God's act of creation as one of ordering according to number, measure, and weight. Evidently, Hrotsvit considers the creative act to consist of establishing order, setting up precise harmony in the organization of materials and presenting, thus, a striking analogy to divine creation.

Linkage exists on the literal, metaphoric, and thematic levels; it occurs between lines and segments of the same work, between works of the same group (that is, legends, or dramas), and between works of different groups. The more pronounced correspondences exist between groups of works dealing with similar themes: the legends and the dramas, both utilizing the hagiographic plots, on the one hand, and the epics dealing with historical subject matter on the other. While these echoes might be described, on the technical level, as instances of amplification or expolition, that is, the recapturing of the subject from different angles to insure reader compliance, the exact balance of the recurrences between male and female protagonists serves the additional purpose of definition, of the schematization of an ideal applicable to both sexes. In this manner, the formal and thematic redoubling not only underlines unity of intent and the clear perception of all the works as an organic whole, but it also effects a kind of hermeneutic retake: a rereading of hagiographic plots which encourages an accretion of meaning or even reinterpretation, in novel, even strange generic environments.

The initial linkage between the legends and the dramas is effected by the person of Agnes, heroine of the last legend, at whose grave and at whose intercession Constantia, heroine of the first legend, is healed from the double evil of leprosy and paganism. The dramas, like the legends, are linked by double treatment of plots: the two *passiones*, *Dulcitius* and *Sapientia*, deal with the persecution and martyrdom of three allegorical sisters; *Abraham* and *Paphnutius* repeat the fall and conversion theme; *Gallicanus* and *Calimachus* center on the theme of conversion.

The two epics, *Gesta Oddonis Imperatori* and *Primordia*, concern members of the Saxon dynasty in their roles as secular rulers (*Gesta*) and religious rulers/benefactors (*Primordia*). The 34-hexameter-line poem on the Apocalypse of Saint John links the legends and dramas (both hagiographic in theme and liturgical in language) on the one hand, and the epics (heroic/historic in theme, more secular in language) on the other, by providing description for the twelve murals of the abbey of Gander-sheim. The iconographic significance, hagiographic relevance and his-toric importance of Saint John are linked in his role as patron of Gandersheim and the inspiration of the abbey's founding.

The legends and the dramas are linked individually as well. The four treatments of the fall and conversion theme (*Theophilus, Basilius, Abra-ham, Paphnutius*) all exemplify the doctrine of heavenly grace for the repentant sinner, the *misericordia* of Christ and his saints. In the legends men lapse; in the dramas women do. In the legends men sell their immortal souls to the devil for earthly gain; in the dramas women sell their bodies to men for gain. In all four treatments, sinners are helped by a member of the opposite sex who is related to them in two of the treatments and unrelated in the other two. In *Basilius* it is the servant's wife who takes the initiative and requests Bishop Basilius's help for the miserable sinner; in *Abraham* it is Maria's uncle who sets out on the long journey to reclaim his lapsed niece. In *Theophilus* the Virgin Mary intercedes for the repentant Theophilus; in *Paphnutius* the saintly hermit of the desert seeks out the famous courtesan Thais in order to convert her.

The four *passiones* exemplify the same sex-inversion. Pelagius and Dionysius are male martyrs, the heroines of *Dulcitius* and *Sapientia* are young girls. The sex of the persecutors, however, never varies: all four are male pagan rulers. All four plots involve the persecution of Christian by pagan; all four contain miracles of Christ's aid to his witnesses. Both *Pelagius* and *Dulcitius* introduce subplots dealing with illicit love and heroically resisted seduction; in both, the protagonists' chastity is con-trasted with the antagonists' promiscuity. Both *Dionysius* and *Sapientia* develop plots in which the persecution is triggered by the protagonists' missionary activity which the pagan rulers see as social, religious and political subversion. In *Dionysius* Domitian is angered because his sub-jects flock to the bishop to be baptized; in *Sapientia* the reason for Antiochus's denunciation of Sapientia is her great missionary zeal to persuade Roman women of the importance of abstinence – Antiochus is outraged because, following Sapientia's preachings, wives no longer share their husbands' table and bed.

Gongolf and *Agnes*, exemplifying the remunerative and punitive as-pects of divine justice, correspond to *Gallicanus* and *Calimachus*. *Cali-machus*, like *Gongolf*, treats of a married saint – Gongolf and Drusiana are the only two married saints in Hrotsvit's legends and dramas. Both of them, however, live in synesaictical marriage. Both plots involve adulter-ous lust and the death of the protagonists because of the antagonists' illicit passion. In *Calimachus*, however, Drusiana is miraculously resurrected and Calimachus is converted at her grave, while Gongolf's adulterous wife (as Fortunatus) persists in her iniquity. Again, the sex roles of the protagonists are reversed in the drama: Gongolf, the male virtuous hero of the legend, dies because of the guiles of his lascivious wife and her lover; Drusiana, the virtuous heroine of the drama, is pursued by a handsome youth possessed by adulterous lust.

Agnes and *Gallicanus* both concern the preservation of the heroine's virginity and her vow to the Heavenly Bridegroom. In both treatments the offer to be avoided is of honorable marriage; likewise in both plots the would-be lovers/husbands are later converted and bear testimony for Christ the Savior. This is the only instance of a double treatment of a theme where the sex roles are not reversed: the preservation of one's virginity appears to be a paradigmatically female virtue. In three of the four treatments of the theme the protagonists become catalysts of salvation for their would-be lovers/husbands. In *Gongolf*, the only version with a male protagonist, however, the catalytic role does not succeed but exacerbates the wife's iniquity.

While the linkages of the epics to the legends and dramas are less pronounced, they do nevertheless exist. The historical persons of the two epics are idealized and romanticized so that they resemble the hagiographic heroes and heroines of the legends and of the plays. Otto I, hero of the *Gesta Oddonis*, is the ideal Christian ruler. He is the pious, benevolent and diplomatic hero, resembling Gongolf and the Emperor Constantine of Gallicanus and marked, as they are, by his *iusticia* and *misericordia*, and Otto's designations (like those of Gongolf, Pelagius, and Dionysius) link him with God and his saints. In the *Primordia*, Gerberga is the living embodiment of the love of chastity and of the resolute and unchanging will with which she faces the temptations of the world. Like Agnes, Mary, and Constantia, Gerberga also refuses to marry her bridegroom, Bernhard, because she has taken a secret vow of chastity. Oda, ancestress of the Liudolf dynasty, is the shining example of virtuous motherhood. Like Sapientia, she survives the deaths of her daughters (except for Christina's), all of whom she encourages in their religious endeavors.

The last text attributed to Hrotsvit, *Lives of the Popes Anastasius and Innocent*, is no longer extant.

Hrotsvit's protagonists in all her works are the saints and the Liudolfs. Her texts seek adherence to the monastic ideal and to an epistemology which confirms that truth, that is revealed truth, is recognizable, absolute, eternal and imitable; a truth persuasively conveyed for the moral edification of her readers.

Works

Preface to the Legends

I offer this little book,/ small in stylistic merits, but not small in the efforts it took/ to the good will of the wise/ for correction and advice/ at least to those who don't enjoy to rail/ against authors who fail,/ but, rather, prefer to correct the work's flaws. I do confess/ that my failings are rather more than less/ in the handling of meter, style, and diction,/ and that there is much in these works warranting correction./ Yet, the one admitting openly her failing/ should find forgiveness prevailing/ and her mistakes deserve kind help. When, however, the charge is raised/ – or at least by some so appraised –/ that parts of this work's discourses/ are based on apocryphal sources,/ then I must reply/ and hereby testify/ that it was not a misdeed of presumption/ but the innocent error of flawed assumption,/ because when I first started to weave the strands of these works, I was not aware that some of my sources met with doubt;/ and when I did find this out,/ I still decided not to suppress them because what appears to be false today/ may perhaps be proven true another day./ As it is, I am in dire need/ for the support and help of many indeed/ especially because I lacked all confidence and strength when I first started/ and these verses crafted/ as I was neither mature in years nor sufficient in learning./ Neither did I dare consult the discerning/ and show my drafts to the wise/ or ask them for advice/ so as not to be prohibited from writing on account of my rusticity. Thus, I first began to compose in secret, all alone/ struggling to write, then destroying what was poorly done,/ trying to the best of my ability, and with all my might/ to put together a text – be its merit ever so slight –/ using the writings I was able to gather here, in our Gandersheim Abbey.

I was first taught by Riccardis, the wisest and kindest of teachers, and by others thereafter, who continued my education/ and then, finally, by my lady of high station/ Gerberga of royal blood, my merciful abbess, under whose rule I now live. She is younger in years than I, but as befits the Emperor's niece, more advanced in learning./ It was she, who, other authors concerning/ continued my instruction/ offering me an introduction/ to the works of those writers whom she herself studied with learned men.

However difficult and arduous and complex/ metrical composition may appear for the fragile female sex,/ I, persisting/ with no one assisting/ still put together my poems in this little work/ not relying on my own powers and talents as a clerk/ but always trusting in heavenly grace's aid/

for which I prayed,/ and I chose to sing them in the dactylic mode/ so that my talent, however tiny, should not erode,/ that it should not lie dormant in my heart's recesses and be destroyed by slothful neglect's corrosion,/ but that, struck by the mallet of eager devotion,/ it bring forth a tiny little sound of divine praise/ and, thus, if for no other purpose but for this case,/ it may be transformed into an instrument of some utility/ regardless of the limits of my ability./

Therefore, reader, whoever you may be,/ if you live rightly/ and are wise in God, don't withhold the favor of your benign goodwill from these flawed pages/ that are not built on the authorities of precedent or the wisdom of sages./ If, by chance, you find here something well wrought, give all credit to God's grafting/ but for all the flaws, assign the blame to my poor crafting./ Do this, however, not by viciously attacking or by begrudging/ but by indulgently judging,/ because the force of the censoring lance is broken/ when, at the onset, humble words of confession are spoken./

Dutch = Kingly

Basilius

He who wants to learn   and by sure proof discern
God's mercy and the Lord's   many and great rewards,
With humble heart and meek,   these small verses should read.
Scorn he should not render   at the writer's weaker gender
Who these small lines had sung   with a woman's untutored tongue,
But, rather should he praise   the Lord's celestial grace
Who wants not that in due pain   sinners their punishment gain,
But eternal life He grants   to the sinner who repents.
This shall be proven here;   thus, shall he rejoice in cheer
Whoever these verses reads   and the present account heeds.

At the time when Basilius[1]   (famous for his virtues)
Our holy Church guided   and in just rule presided
As Bishop of Caesarea,   elected to that see,
There lived in that place   a man of illustrious race.
Proterius was his name,   he was of noble fame;
Honored by young and old,   he was, too, rich in gold.
A single child he had,   one of the female sex
(No other child was there   to be his riches' heir).
He loved this only child   with devotion tender and mild,
And hoped in love paternal   and in fear of God eternal
For this virtuous goal: that the girl's immortal soul
Forever adorned would be   with gems of perfect virginity,
Rather than that her earthly form   be decked out in worldly pomp.
Therefore, he took good care   that she be with virgins fair,
Who to Jesus consecrated   and with holy veil elated
In the cloister's confines   spend their godly lives.

Yet the author of all evil,   seducer of man primeval,
This just father's laudable vow   detested and planned to disallow.
He caused a servant of the sire   to burn in mad desire
For the daughter's love,   the girl mentioned above.[2]

---

[1] Basilius was archbishop of Caesarea from 370 to 379; Hrotsvit used the Latin version of the
Greek *vita* (translated by Ursus) for her legend. See Homeyer, *Hrotsvithae Opera*, p. 174.
My translation of "Basilius" first appeared in K. M. Wilson, ed., *Medieval Women Writers*
(Athens: University of Georgia Press, 1984).
[2] Hrotsvit used the term *servus* to describe the young man. In the early Middle Ages *servus*

This miserable swain,   by love's arrows slain,
Pined and pined away,   the more he burned in pain.
He knew himself unworthy   for such an exalted union;
Thus, he dared not reveal   his heart's hurt and zeal;
But after searching around,   a magician at last he found
To whom, hoping for gain,   the secret of his pain
And bitter sadness told.   He promised gifts and gold
If the magician could bind   the daughter's tender heart
To the servant's affection   and in equal passion.
This perverse friend of fraud   then to the youth thus spoke.[3]
"I don't believe I hold   the power so bold
To join a high-born lady   as consort to her slave;
But if according to my way   you're willing to obey
The prince of eternal dark   to whose commands I hark,
Then he can quickly act   and your desires grant
If only nevermore   Christ's name you will adore."

Blinded by mad craze,   his heart with passion ablaze,
The wretched youth agreed   and to all his consent decreed.
The magician then wrote   to his master this note:
"Prince of infernal hell,   great ruler of the deep,
Your servants are always eager   to seduce and lead to evil
Those who were cleansed by the font   of baptism, and from the flock
Of Christ are departed   and now to you are charted,
So that your fellowship's size   be always on the rise.
Today I send this youth   greatly rejoicing in truth,
For as soon as you conspire   to fulfill his secret desire,
You shall incur for sure   a servant for the future."
Then the magician gave   this note to the poor youth
. . .

At night,   over the tomb of a heathen
. . .

The young man was all eager   to follow the evil intriguer,
And to the spot he turned   to which the magician referred

and *sclavus* were often used interchangeably, but by the tenth century modifiers such as *saracenus* were added in order to assure the audience that only infidels could be slaves. Hrotsvit's concern here is less with the actual position of the young man than with the inappropriateness of the union between two people of entirely different socioeconomic backgrounds.

3   The magician is described as *perversus amicus*; he receives his magical powers from the devil. Thus, his craft becomes the perversion of the divine power to work miracles.

So he may ask for aid   from the ancient snake,
Who always tempts his friends   to destruction's ends.
Without any delay   hell's servants came his way
And led the erring boy   gloating with malicious joy
To the cruel seat   of the dark spirits' meet.
There the author of all fraud   and of all crime and feud,
The damnable champion   of the contemptible legion,
Was seated in their group   circled by his dark troop.
There traps he prepares   for wretches unawares,
And forever he compiles   insidious plans and guiles.
There he studies the wrong   committed by all his throng.[4]

When he had carefully read   the note that the magician sent,
Like a lion he roared   and in fury thus deplored
(In his savage rage   he terrified the poor youth):[5]
"Never do you stay   faithful to me, you Christians,
But as soon as I ordain   your desire to obtain,
Then promptly you flee   and to Christ take your plea.
Me you desire and scorn   after the gifts I had borne,
And full trust you embrace   in Christ's mercy and grace,
Because He's willing to grant   to those who repent
His forgiveness sublime   regardless of the crime.
Therefore, if you desire   the lawful embrace to acquire
Of your master's child,   then you must deny Christ
And also holy baptism   that Christ gave to His people.
And you must agree   forever to belong to me
And always to remain   in eternal infernal pain.
Give me then a note   by your own hand wrought
And I shall quickly act   to show my might's effect."

By these speeches captivated,   the poor servant soon abated
And signed with happy heart   his own damnation's chart.
He gave without fear   his soul to the hellish fiend.
Joyful with the affirmation   of the servant's sure damnation,
The fiend in happy mood   soon sent his hellish brood
So that they could incite   the poor virgin's plight,
And make her burn in sinful passion   for her own servant.

---

4   That is, Satan makes his inquiries as to whether the planned evil plots have been executed.
5   The raging lion imagery is almost invariably associated with unjust rulers: pagan princes and the devil.

As soon as her fragile heart   by love's charms was beguiled,
This offspring of a noble house   desired to be his spouse.
And she exclaimed aloud   that to him she wished to be bound.
Her father she addressed   with these words of request:
"Sweetest father mild,   have mercy with your daughter
And give me right over   to the youth whom I love
So I may not die   in languishing desire!"
Her plea the father heard   and with bitter tears returned:
"Alas, alas, what's this,   sole hope of your father?
Tell me who caused this pain   and turned your head with flatteries vain?
And who had done this wrong   and deceived you with a honeyed tongue?
Have I not made a vow   to give you an exalted bough
And pledged you with pride   to be Christ's heavenly bride?
With chaste heart forever,   him alone you were to honor
And sing His praise and glory   together with the celestial choir,
So when freed from death   you may join the virginal band!
But now you burn in affection   for a lascivious servant's passion.
With voice soft and mild   I beg you, my child,
Please, avoid such craze   and stultitude so base.
Else you will bring us shame   and all your ancestors defame.
But if you insist to retain   this evil wish insane,
Then, sweet daughter, may you perish   and in disgrace soon vanish."

Yet she scorned with spite   the father's good advice
And resisting her father,   she thus complained further:
"If you delay to act   and my wish not quickly grant,
Then soon you shall repent   and your child's death lament."
Forced by her bitter plaint,   not freely, but constrained,
The father joined them both   and his child to the slave betrothed.
He also gave them freely   a substantial dowry.
When they were to part,   he said with embittered heart:
"Daughter forlorn,   of luckless parents born,
Once honor but now shame   to the mother who bore you.
You brought foul disgrace   to our ancestral race.
Go now and rejoice   in your darling servant;
But later you shall grieve   and due punishment receive."
 When the marriage vows were taken,   so fraught by the fraud of Satan,
Then it pained Christ the King   who salvation to us did bring,
That those whom He had saved   and with His precious blood redeemed
Should in the enemy's chain   as captives still remain.
It pleases Christ to aid   even those renegade.
Soon the servant's wife,   erring in her life,

Was told that her husband   was not a good Christian,
And that he never set   his foot on the Church's step,
That he signed himself over   to the greedy serpent's power,
And the true faith denied   and Christ's name maligned.
When with her own ears   she heard of his atrocious deeds,
The poor wife concluded   that she had been deluded.
She began to tremble   and with lifeless members
She fell to the floor;   her hair anon she tore,
And she beat her breast   with her fists without rest.
With bitter tears and sighs   she addressed the skies;
"Those who do not heed   when dear parents plead
Shall never be saved.   This has been proven here.
Alas, alas, the light   at birth why did I sight,
And why was I not enclosed   in dark sepulchral vaults,
So, thus, I would have missed   falling in death's abyss!"

While she so commented   and sadly lamented,
Suddenly her husband came,   criminal and full of blame.
He quickly swore an oath   that all this was not in troth,
But she responded thus   to his repeated denials:
"If you are, by and large,   innocent of the charge,
Then come with me to Church   tomorrow morn, I urge,
And there the Holy Mass   celebrate with me."
By her sound reason defeated[6]   the husband then conceded
And told her the true cause   of how the deed arose.
Then she did not abide,   but put womanly weakness aside
And summoned manly strength   to her prudent heart.
She hurried to the house   of the saintly Basilius
And at his sacred feet   prostrate she did entreat
And poured forth this moan   from her disturbed soul:
"Saintly man of God,   succor us poor sinners,
And save us from the grasp   of the savage fiend
Who already unfolds   the perish of our souls!"
When she had gotten rid   of this weighty sin,
The bishop of the Lord   the wretched servant implored.
He began to inquire,   in benevolent desire,
Whether after his dissent,   he were willing to repent

---

[6]   That is, the husband, having made a pact with the devil, naturally cannot take communion
  – her "sound reason" is the attempt to persuade him to take communion to prove his
  innocence or expose his guilt.

And to Christ return.   The servant said he yearned
For his salvation greatly –   yet he despaired of mercy:
"I committed the crime,   of free will I signed
With my hand the letters   that gave me to the fiend in fetters.
With my heart turned blind   Christ's name I denied."
The man of God then said: "You don't need to dread
Your future, nor doubt   that divine grace shall abound,
Because God's only Son,   the mildest judge of all,
Has never turned away   a repentant sinner;
If you rue your sins,   he will grant you help.
Relinquish thus the depth   of sin that brings only death,
And flee to the safe haven   of divine mercy and love.
That haven grants its shores   to all who approach."
With these admonitions   and with the servant's permission
The bishop set him right   and had him in a cell confined
So Christ he might implore   and his enormous sins deplore.

After three days went by,   the bishop came to inquire
How the sinner bore   the penance and pain.
The servant, greatly exhausted,   with these words responded:
"I can hardly bear   the punishment of dark spirits,
They beat me and tear me   with continuous strokes,
And besiege me ceaselessly   with hard and heavy stones.
Mostly they oppose me   and bitterly reproach me
Because to them I came   and of free will became
One of theirs. Never   did they force me to surrender."
Then the learned healer   and languishing souls' redeemer
Caused him to be fed   and away he sped.
Some days later he came   to visit the sinner again,
And ask him how he fared   in the chamber dark.
The servant then said: "Good father I now fared
Much better, for I hear   those voices from afar."
Heartily delighted,   Basilius departed
After refreshing him more   just as he did before.
Forty days then passed,   and the bishop came again;
Awhile the penitent   bewailed his bitter sins.
Basilius found him glad   whom he expected to be sad,
And he greatly wondered   and the happy change so pondered.
Through bitter tears now cleansed   the sinner the bishop addressed
And said that he was sure   divine forgiveness to procure:
"I hope I shall be saved,   and through you redeemed
Because, dreaming, at night   I saw you in a fight

With the savage snake   battling for my sake.
I saw that the fiend retreated   with divine force defeated."

Listening intently,   the bishop heard these words
And sang the loud praise   of Christ's heavenly grace.
He removed the captive   from the chamber dark
To his own small chambers   next to holy Church
So in the bishop's cell   for the night he would dwell.
Then the bishop ordered   the faithful to assemble,
So with him all night   in prayer they unite
And the good shepherd implore   to rejoin once more
The lost sheep to the flock   as it is his wont.
When the sun emerged   and the black shadows dispersed,
The bishop firmly grasped   the sinner by his right
And to the Church he led   the servant by the hand.
When they touched the threshold   of the sacred house,
From a hidden spot   the demon darted forth.
Intent on hidden harm,   he snatched the man's left arm
And pulled with curses coarse   the servant with great force.
But Basilius discharged   his office with great might:
"Let go, you thief," he scorned,   "This creature of the Lord!
Conquered now you lay;   so give back your prey!"
The hellish fiend replied,   the enemy to all,
Filling the air with a howl   and with his perverse growl:
"How dare you say   you take my slave away
Who out of free will   submitted to my chains?
The written agreement   that he gave to me
I shall bring to show   on the final day of law."
The saintly bishop spoke   and gave him this reply:
"By Christ's command, I trust,   that equitable judge,
You shall soon relinquish   the letters that you hold."
After he had spoken,   the whole flock of the faithful
Began with pious hearts   to praise the Almighty
And to entreat His aid   for their shepherd's crusade
Against the savage fiend.   Anon the hellish writ
Fell from above and lay   right in the bishop's way.

Then the folk rejoiced   and with their bishop joint
They all began to raise   their voices and praise
Christ the benign, who showed   His usual compassion
And rescued the captive   from the lion's jaws.
To heaven let us raise   our voices and thus praise

And laud the Lord Christ   with our happy hearts,
He has kindly bequeathed us   hope for grace and mercy,
To Him all glory be rend   and honor without end,
All praise and victory   be His eternally, AMEN.

Pelagius

Peerless Pelagius,[1] thou fearless martyr of Christ!
Soldier, loyal and strong, of Him who's eternally Lord.
Look with gracious regard, on her who's thy humble, poor servant.
Devoted to thee in her heart and cherishing thee in her mind.
Be mindful of Hrotsvit thy maid and to her song, too, lend thy kind aid.[2]
Grant thou, I pray, that my mind's dark and unlit recesses,
Sprinkled with dew from above, be moistened gently with love,
That I may worthily sing and the tale of thy marvels depict,
And that my pen may acclaim thy triumphs and also thy fame,
Tell how in death thou hast conquered, the blood-thirsty world in the end
And how, with your precious sweet blood, you purchased the glorious
  palm.

In the Western part of the world there glowed an ornament bright,
A city famous in lore, proud of its new might at war
It throve under the reign of colonists from Spain.
Cordoba was its name; wealthy it was and of fame;[3]
Well known for its pleasures and for its splendid treasures
Held, too, in great esteem, for the seven-forked stream
Of learning. Also in the fore for its great triumphs at war.
Once this famous town to Christ in faith was bound
And gave its sons to God, cleansed in the baptismal font
But suddenly a martial force changed the well-established course
And laws of holy faith, by spreading through the state
Errors of false dogma, harming the faithful folk.
For the faithless tribe of unrestrained Saracens
Fell upon the stout people of this town.

---

1 *Pelagius*, unlike Hrotsvit's other legends, is not based on a written source but on eyewitness
   reports. It has been suggested that perhaps a member of Emperor Otto's embassy to Abderrahman provided Hrotsvit with the details of the new martyr. The legend is composed in leonine
   hexameters (that is, dactylic hexameters with internal rhyme or, more frequently, homoeoteleuton) and ornamented with the frequent use of hyperbaton, alliteration, antonomasia,
   and litotes. This is a revised version of my translation which first appeared in Elizabeth Petroff,
   Medieval Women's Visionary Literature (New York, Oxford: Oxford University Press, 1986).
2 Hrotsvit records her name six times in her works (Epistola; Preface to the epics; *Maria*, line
   18; *Ascensio*, line 148; *Gongolf*, line 3; *Pelagius*, line 3). She herself translates her Old Saxon
   name as "Ego Clamor Validus" – the "Forceful Voice."
3 Hrotsvit spells the city's name "Corduba."

They seized by force   the reign of this glorious domain,
And murdered the good king,   who, cleansed by holy baptism,
Held the royal scepter   by right and with might;
And ruled his men for long   with just restraints and laws.
Vanquished now he lay,   by hostile swords, and they
Who survived the carnage,   were now a conquered folk.
The leader of the barbaric tribe,   the author of the strife,
A person quite perverse,   in life and customs cursed,
Seized for himself the entire   glorious and splendid Empire.
He settled his wicked allies   in the wasted country
And filled the mourning city   with many a foe
Polluting thus this place   of pure and ancient faith
Through barbarian customs,   how sad to say,
By mixing his pagans   with the faithful natives
So they may urge the Christians   to give up the old customs
And stain themselves, like he,   through cults of pagan worship.
But the gentle crowd,   whom Christ the shepherd ruled,
Scorned the doleful orders   of the sinful tyrant,
Saying they'd rather die   and with Christ's law comply
Than survive, and serve   his foolish cult absurd.
The king having learned this,   realized in full
That it would bring him harm   if he did not change his mind
And put all wealthy people   to death in this rich town
Which he had just now captured   in valiant fighting.[4]
Therefore he decided   to change the first decree
And issued a pronouncement   to such a new effect,
That whoever so desired   to serve the eternal King
And desired to honor   the customs of his sires,
Might do so without fear   of any retribution.
Only a single condition,   he set to be observed,
Namely that no dweller   of the aforesaid city
Should presume to blaspheme   the golden idol's name
Whom this prince adored   or whoever else was king.
Or else, it was so willed,   this man was promptly to be killed,
And had to bear the sentence   of punishment by death.
Following these decrees,   calm in apparent peace,
The faithful city was weighed   down with a thousand evils.
But those whom their desire   for Christ's love set on fire,
And whom the thirst for martyrdom   urged to insult and scorn

---

4   Since he cannot tax Muslims, the caliph needs a well-to-do class of Christians for his tax base.

Those images of marble   which, with jewels adorned,
The prince with prostrate body,   adored with frankincense,
These men's bodies perished   at the prince's orders,
But their souls, purified,   heavenwards repaired.
Many years so passed,   and amongst vicissitudes
Cordoba since that time   was subject to pagan kings.
Then in our own days   an offspring of that race
Assumed in succession,   the reign of his fathers.
He was worse than they,   and stained with wantonness,
And called Abderrahman,   haughty with his kingship's glory.[5]
He treated the Christians,   in his fathers' manner
And enforced the law   concerning their faith.
He did not abolish   through kindness the harsh edict
Which the author of woe,   the city's cruel foe
Once had ordained   as he vanquished the town.
But mindful of the law   and in his heart aglow
He drenched with guiltless blood,   frequently the land
Ending the holy lives,   thus, of those just men,
Who were burning to chant   the sweet praise of Christ
And were eager to denounce   the king's own foolish idols.
This sacrilegious king   showed such pride at court,
(earning great punishments,   well deserved, much later)
That he even boasted   to be the King of Kings
And boasted that all nations   were subject to his rule
And that no tribe was ever   filled so with strength and valor
That they would dare to smite   his army in a fight.
As he was, more than lawful,   puffed up in arrogance
He heard of a nation   living in the region
Of far-away Galicia,   quite excellent in war,
Worshipping the true Christ   and making war on idols
Who freely dared to spurn   his decrees and laws
And refused to be serving   masters so clearly undeserving.
Hearing this, set afire,   the king burned with demonic ire.
And in his heart, awake,   was the bile of the ancient snake.
In his mind he wondered,   and craftily he pondered
How he would deal a blow,   and destroy such a foe.
He disclosed at length   to all his ill intent

---

5   Abd-ar-Rahman, Caliph of Cordoba. Here Hrotsvit emphasizes the regressivity of dynamic
    succession in direct contrast to her depiction of the (Christian) Liudolfs' progressive
    evolution as an ever better paradigm of virtue and political power.

And addressed the nobles   of that wealthy city
Barking such evil words   from his pestiferous maw[6]
"It is not a secret   that kings have submitted to us
And that all the nations   that the deep sea surrounds
Live in accordance   and submission to our laws.
But what bold confidence   drives the subject Galicians
That they would have foresworn   and our treaties clearly scorn,
Ungrateful for past kindness,   I simply do not know.
What we'll have to do,   thus, is attack Galicia
Harassing with armed forces   those insurgent foes,
Until before our weapons,   prostrate, against their will
They submit their necks   forever to our chains."
After he had boasted,   and his evil intent revealed,
He ordered that, in quick time,   arranged in rank and file
The folk should gather   provided with arms and banners
So that, joined with him,   they should destroy that tribe.
He displayed his face   under his bejeweled helmet,
Iron armor decking   his wanton and lewd limbs.
He engaged the Galicians   in a first encounter,
And promptly he chanced to gain   and such a triumph obtain
That he trapped twelve nobles   and captured their lord,
Seizing all these men   and putting them in chains.
With their nobles taken,   the faithful nation, shaken,
After much fierce fighting   surrendered to the foe,
And submitted to the fold   of the perverse lord.
Then, the treaty, too   was restored anew,
And twelve captive nobles   set forth in their chains
With their fellow captive,   the leader of that nation.
The nobles were set free   quite soon from their fetters
Ransomed at high prices   drawn on their wealth,
But on the king's command,   the duke's ransom was doubled,
To a sum exceeding   what he could pay just then:
And when he bore as ransom   to the greedy ruler
Whatever of treasures   he could find at home,
By some mishap it was   less than the demanded sum.
This the king declined,   fostering fraud in mind,
And refused to return   the sweet duke to his people;

---

6   The animal imagery is quite pronounced in these lines. Usually applied to the Devil and his
cohorts (cf. *Basilius*), animal imagery is also frequently associated with the infidels in
Hrotsvit's works.

Until, in full, he was told,　he'd pay the required gold.
The king acted thus,　not just in his greed
But in his desire strong,　to kill the nation's lord.

The duke had an only son,　of illustrious descent,
Endowed with every charm　of body and of shape.
Pelagius by name,　elegant and lustrous;
Prudent in council,　replete with all the virtues.
He barely had completed　the years of his boyhood
And had just now reached　the first blossoms of youth.
When he learned the king's　treatment of his father
He coaxed his grieving sire　with such caressing words:
"Oh my dear father,　hear my speech with kindness
And, to what I implore thee,　please be well disposed.
I am quite aware that　thy years are now declining,
And that thy strength now lacks　its accustomed vigor.
Thou can bear no labor,　however slight it be;
I, on the other hand,　can cope with all demands
And can with limbs still strong　submit me to a most cruel lord.
Therefore I entreat thee　and with prayers beseech thee
That as a pledge thou bring　me to the pagan king,
Until thou can furnish　the ransom gold in full,
Or thou may die, gray haired,　in narrow fetters snared."

But the old man pled　and with stern voice thus said:
"Cease such speech sweet son,　cease such speech my dear,
Or your gray-haired father　may promptly die for grief.
My very life's dependent　wholly on your welfare,
And without you, my dear,　I couldn't live a day.
You are all my glory,　splendor of our fathers,
You the only hope, too,　for our conquered nation.
Therefore it is better　if I leave our country
And enter proud Spain　as a captive in chains,
Than that you take my place,　destroying all my hopes."
Pelagius, however,　heeded not his father
But with honeyed words　he coaxed his sire's mind
And forced him so at length　to yield to intent pleas.
The venerable father　finally agreed
And delivered as hostage　his son, the wretched boy.
The king then gave the order　that Pelagius cross the border
And returned rejoicing,　as victor to his land.

No one, though, should credit   this to the king's own merit,[7]
That he should have succeeded   in such a splendid way,
But rather the reason lies,   and with God the Judge resides
Whose secret plan was either   that this tribe, so chastised,
Should beweep the sins   of which they all stood charged,
Or that Pelagius   be killed for faith in Christ,
And might thus reach the spot,   where to die was his lot,
And pour forth the waters there   of his blood for Christ,
Giving his soul to God,   made holy by his death.[8]

When this savage king   had entered his rich city
Bearing the victory   over the faithful tribe,
He instantly ordered   that Christ's illustrious friend
Be bound and then thrown   into a dark prison
And be fed but little food   he who was used to plenitude.
Cordoba has a place,   foul and under vaults
Oblivious to light,   consigned to deep darkness,
Source of great suffering,   they say, to poor wretches.
Hereto Pelagius,   distinguished son of peace
Was confined by the king's   strict and wicked orders.
Hereto came eagerly   the foremost men of town
Moved by care humane,   to soften the youth's grave pain.
As they beheld the grace   of the captive's lovely face
And as they had tasted, each,   of the sweetness of his speech
And heard words embellished,   with the honey of rhetoric
Then they all desired   to free him from his bondage.
They wished to be kind   and change the ruler's mind.
As they knew for sure   of the great allure
And the burning passion,   that the city's lord
Stained by pederasty   felt for handsome youths,
With whom to join he longed   in friendship's tender bond,
They felt encouraged to hope   for the boy's salvation.
With pity in their hearts,   they pleaded with the king:
"Bravest prince, it is not proper   nor becoming for you to order
That such a handsome youth   be punished so harshly,
And that the tender arms   of this guiltless boy be fettered.

---

7   Hrotsvit's authorial intervention makes sure that the reader does not wonder about divine injustice.

8   Pelagius thus becomes a martyr both of faith and of virginity as well as a paradigm of self-sacrifice. His rewards in heaven are also threefold: he is rewarded as witness of the faith, as a virgin, and as a loving son.

If you would ever deign   to behold his splendor
And would taste the flow   of his honeyed speech
You would then desire   to join him to yourself
And to have him take on   the rank of officer,
So in his dazzling beauty,   he might serve at court.
The king, much mollified   and roused by this speech
Ordered that Pelagius   be freed from his bonds
And his body be cleansed   with pure and clean water
And his body be decked   in rich and purple garments
And his neck adorned   with a jeweled necklace
So he thus be brought   to that well-wrought court.
Following the king's   arrogant command
The martyr was released   promptly from black prison
And dressed in splendid attire   was presented to the sire.

Now as he was placed   in the midst of courtiers,
He surpassed them all   in beauty of countenance.
They were all amazed   as at him they gazed
Admiring now his face,   now his sweet speech.
The king, too, felt delight   at the youth's lovely sight,
And enflamed with love   for the royal offspring's beauty,
He ordered a squire   that the object of his desire,
Pelagius, be placed   on the throne with him,
Fervently desiring   the youth's proximity.
As he bent his head,   he tried to steal kisses
From the desired youth,   embracing his sweet neck
But Christ's valiant soldier   would clearly disavow
Such love from a pagan   so stained by lechery
So playfully he turned   his ear to the king's lips
Denying him thus,   amidst much mirth, his mouth.
While, with his lovely lips,   he spoke these fearless words:
"It is not fit for a man   cleansed by Christian baptism
To submit his chaste neck   to barbarous embrace,
Neither is it meet   for a one with chrism anointed
To entice the kiss   of an idol's lewd servant
Therefore embrace those fools   with your uncurbed heart
Who, like you, appease   those foolish earthen gods.
Those men be your lovers,   who serve the stupid idols."
But the king responded,   not moved to any anger,
Softly he tried to calm   the beloved youth;
"Oh you foolish boy,   you boast that you can toy
And scorn, without punishment   the kindness of our law

And dare to make such sport   with our gods at court.
Are you not moved to bend,   knowing your young life must end
And that you will make childless   your grieving parents?
We kill those who assault   and blaspheme our cult,
We subject them to death   and pierce their throats with swords
Unless they cease their chant   and their blasphemies recant.
I urge you, thus, insisting,   with kind paternal pleading,
That you forbear and limit   such words of savage spirit
And that you join with me   in lasting affection
And from now on not dare   to go against our laws,
But rather with eagerness   obey my royal words,
For you alone I cherish   and you I desire to honor
With great magnificence   before all others at court;
You'll be second only   to me in this great kingdom."
Thus he spoke and with his right   he held the martyr's face,
Embracing with his left   the martyr's sacred neck,
So that thus he may place   at last a single kiss.
But the martyr thwarted   the king's shrewd playful act
And swung at the king's lips   promptly with his fist.
He dealt such a blow   to the king's face below
That the blood gushing forth   from the inflicted wound
Stained the king's beard   and wetted all his garments.
Then the king was moved   and to great anger provoked,
And ordered that Pelagius,   child of heaven's King,
Be thrown over the walls   and hurled from an engine
Which, when used in war,   threw rocks at the foe,
So that the noble martyr,   dashed on the river's shore
(Which with its mighty waves   surrounded the city)
Be broken in all members   and so meet his death.[9]
The king's haughty servants   obeyed his cruel words
And promptly they performed   this unheard-of punishment,
Throwing from a sling   Pelagius to be martyred
Across the very tall   ramparts of that town.
But even though large masses   of rocks stood in the way
Obstructing much the fall   of the martyr's glorious body,
Nevertheless Christ's friend   stayed totally unharmed.
Promptly, of course, the news   was brought to the royal ears
That the body of the martyr   could not, as he had ordered,

---

[9] It is curious that Pelagius is first hurled from a war machine rather than beheaded as
prescribed by the edict. Perhaps Abderrahman wishes to destroy his beauty as well.

Be torn to pieces and rent   by rocks on the river's bank.
Even more furious   because he had been foiled,
The king then gave the order   that the martyr be beheaded
And that so, as he willed,   the punishment be fulfilled.
Promptly the king's henchmen,   trembling at his orders
Killed the faithful youth,   witness of Christ's law
And gave his lifeless body   to the waves to hold.

The soldier of the Heavenly King   destroyed in body by death
Flew swiftly as victor   through the stars to heaven
Borne by heavenly angels   singing hymns and songs.
Then above the stars' height,   seated at the Father's right,
He duly received the palm   from the equitable Judge
For his martyrdom achieved   through laudable death.
He was also granted,   a reward for the love
Which led him to assume   his father's chains for life
And caused him to abandon   his land and his people.
No tongue, indeed, can aspire   to depict with affectionate desire
That beauteous laurel bright,   sparkling with celestial light,
With which he is crowned   for his virginity renowned.
Joined to the chosen throng   of the Heavenly Kingdom,
He sings perpetually   the praise of the Lamb. Amen.

After the executioners   had followed the king's orders,
And had duly committed   the martyr's noble remains
To the bosom of the waters   and placed them among rocks
So the sacred remains   would stay without a tomb,
Christ, who suffers not   that even the tiniest spot
Of hair be harmed of those   who bear witness to His cause
Did not allow His witness   to remain in the stream
But duly He provided   for him a worthy place
Which was to preserve   his holy limbs in a tomb.

It happened that some fishermen,   pounding the waves
With their oars and catching   the wandering fishes
Saw the martyr's limbs   at a distant spot,
Tossing to and fro   amidst the loud waves.
Discerning it from afar   with their careful eyes,
They quickly set sail   and lifted up the body.
They did not recognize   who the person was
Because the limbs despoiled,   with purple blood were soiled,
And his noble head   lay farther down the stream.

Yet they sensed this much   and believed it to be such
That whoever he be,   this man perished for Christ,
Because only those   were condemned to beheading
Who, sprinkled with the waters   of Christian baptism
Did not fear to insult   the king's pagan cult.
When they found the head   and placed it on the shoulders,
They recognized the handsome   face of Pelagius.
Pity in their hearts,   they poured forth these words:
"Alas here lies dead   the sole hope of his nation
And the glory of his land   lies here without a tomb.
Don't we also know   that the remains of those
Whose decapitations   prove them to be Christians,
Can easily be sold   for large amounts of gold?
And who would doubt this   to be the body of a martyr
Since the body lies,   bereft of the head's glory?"
As they were thus talking,   they placed the saint's remains
In their boat's tail.   And quickly they turned sail
And traveled to the port   of that famous city.
Here, after having docked   and their vessel locked,
They sought out in secret   a sacred monastery
Which lay within the walls   surrounding the city.
They carried, hoping for gains,   the blessed martyr's remains
Honored now by all,   to be sold for gold.
The throng of the faithful   received them rejoicing,
And with sweet hymns performed   the sacred funeral rites
They paid generously   a high price to the shipmen
Eager to buy the remains   of the beloved saint.
After they had won   the body for no small sum,
They chose a worthy spot   in which to keep the remains.
Here after the service   had been splendidly performed,
The sacred relics lay   buried under a mound of clay.
Soon the Almighty Lord   of the star bearing court
Made the grave illustrious   through signs miraculous,
So that as the martyr's soul,   that now reigned in heaven,
So, on earth his body   may also reign in glory.

At length the citizens   of the city noticed
That a sizable throng   of men afflicted for long
With diverse diseases,   were here freely healed:
Their loathsome limbs   were cured, without payment.
They were quite perplexed   that this unknown saint
Could be of such merit   as to cause such marvels.

Finally the abbot   and pastor of the people
Pondering the best counsel   in well advised council
Felt that the Lord Most High   must be asked to comply
And be begged sincerely   to reveal to all clearly
The secret of the case   and, thus, remove all doubt.[10]
This plan all people admired   and both men and women desired.
Thus through self-imposed fasting   for three whole days lasting
They solicited the Lord   with hymns and sacred prayers.
With devout hearts   those prayers were performed
And the people thought   that the Heavenly King had been brought
By their effusive prayers   and their eager pleadings
To where he was not opposed   to settle their doubts.
So promptly they prepared   a threatening hot furnace
By heaping up much wood   with united efforts.
When the fire raged   in the stove's huge lap
They took the severed head   of the true servant, of Christ,
Gently speaking such words   of persuasive speech
"Kind King and noble Lord,   ruling the stellar court,
Thou Who knowest to settle   all things in just manner
Cause the merit, Sire,   of the saint to be proved by fire.
If he is indeed   of such virtue and honor
That because of his grace   these gifts of healing take place,
Then cause Thou that the fire   not burn his facial skin
And also that his hair   be totally unharmed.
But, perchance, if he   of lesser merit might be
Then make Thou that be known   by that his skin alone
Be harmed as would be proper   for frail and perishable flesh."
Speaking thus they cast   the glorious head, at last,
For testing, to the waves   of the high surging flames.
And after the full measure   of an hour had passed,
They finally then retrieved   the head from the flames,
Inspecting whether the heat   had harmed the martyr's head.
But the head just glowed   more splendidly than gold
Unharmed and entire,   in spite of the raging fire.
Then the faithful flock   praised with upturned faces
And with sweet melodies   Christ enthroned on high
Who has made resplendent   with many and frequent signs
The mortal relics of those   who died for His cause.

---

[10] Pelagius, being a brand-new saint, must be tested. No other legend of Hrotsvit's contains the description of such a test, for all other legends deal with well-established cults of saints.

Pelagius's relics, as meet,   were placed in a worthy tomb
Where they are venerated   with humble and due respect.
And ever since that day   all doubts were cast away
And the folk rejoiced   in the patron granted them by God.

Preface to the Dramas

Many Catholics one may find,/ and we are also guilty of charges of this kind,/ who for the beauty of their eloquent style,/ prefer the uselessness of pagan guile/ to the usefulness of Sacred Scripture. There are also others, who, devoted to sacred reading and scorning the works of other pagans, yet frequently read Terence's fiction,/ and as they delight in the sweetness of his style and diction,/ they are stained by learning of wicked things in his depiction./[1] Therefore I, the Strong Voice of Gandersheim, have not refused to imitate him in writing/ whom others laud in reading,/ so that in that selfsame form of composition in which the shameless acts of lascivious women were phrased/ the laudable chastity of sacred virgins be praised/ within the limits of my little talent.[2] Not infrequently this caused me to blush/ and brought to my cheeks a scarlet flush,/ because being forced by the conventions of this composition/ I had to contemplate and give a rendition/ of that detestable madness of unlawful lovers and of their evil flattery,/ which we are not permitted even to hear. But had I omitted this out of modesty,/ I would not have fulfilled my intent;/ neither would I have rendered the praise of the innocent/ as well as I could, because the more seductive the unlawful flatteries of those who have lost their sense,/ the greater the Heavenly Helper's munificence/ and the more glorious the victories of triumphant innocence are shown to be,/ especially/ when female weakness triumphs in conclusion./ And male strength succumbs in confusion./ Doubtlessly some will berate/ the worthlessness of this composition as much inferior, much humbler, on a much smaller scale, and not even comparable to the language of him whom I set forth to imitate./ I concede to that; but I say this to my critics: they cannot in fairness reprehend me for considering myself presumptuously yearning/ to be the equal of those who by far are my betters in learning./ For I am not such a braggart nor so presumptuous as to compare

---

[1] Peter Dronke, *Women Writers of the Middle Ages*, pp. 69–70, points out that "none of what Hrotsvitha claims, ostensibly solemnly, at the opening of this Preface can conceivably be literally true . . . that many Catholics (plures . . . Catholici) . . . showed this preference [i.e. for Terence] in Hrotsvitha's time, or had the knowledge to discriminate among styles in this way, is at least a wild exaggeration, and almost certainly a joke."

[2] "Clamor validus Gandeshemensis" is a pun on her Old Saxon name (Hruot = Clamor, suith = validus) as well as a programmatic statement of her authorial intent, aligning herself with John the Baptist (vox clamantis), the patron of Gandersheim Abbey.

myself to the least of these scholars' pupils; this alone I strive for with humble and devoted heart/ – even if aptitude is lacking on my part – / that I may return the gift I received to its Giver again./ For I am not such a lover of myself nor so vain/ that in order to avoid censure I would refrain/ from preaching Christ's glory and strength as it works through His saints to the extent He grants me the ability to do so. If my pious gift pleases anyone, I am glad;/ if, on the other hand,/ it pleases no one, either because of my own worthlessness or the rusticity of my inelegant style,/ then it was still worth the effort for me because while/ I wrote down the trifling efforts of my other works (revealing my lack of knowledge) in the heroic meter's norm,/ here I joined them in the dramatic form,/ always trying to avoid the perilous fetter/ and the dangerous allurement of pagan subject matter./

Her Letter to the Learned Patrons of this Book[1]

To those imbued with learning and abounding in virtue, never jealous of others' success/ but, as befits the truly wise, wishing others the best,/ Hrotsvit, of little learning and worth,/ wishes everlasting joy and present mirth./ I cannot marvel enough at the extent of your laudable conde-scension and I cannot sufficiently requite your magnificent good will and your affection's generous magnitude/ in worthy attestations of gratitude/ on account of my own worthlessness, because you, who are profoundly nourished by the study of philosophy, and have long been the most outstanding among learned men, found the little work of a worthless woman worthy of your admiration,/ and encouraging me with fraternal affection/ you praised the Giver of the grace working through me. You judged me to have a little portion of literary knowledge, whose subtlety far surpassed my woman's intellect. Thus, I barely dared to show/ the rusticity of my little composition's flow/ even to a few and then only to friends, and for this very reason the work almost ceased to grow,/ because just as there were only a few to whom I showed my work, there were not many who gave me encouragement and praise/ either pointing out what was to be corrected or urging me to continue as I had begun my ways./ But now, since the testimony of three is said to constitute truth,[2] invigo-rated by your judgment I will presume to continue my works/ trusting in God and with His permission and to submit it to the examination of learned clerks./ I am torn between two contradictory emotions: joy and fear: I rejoice with all my heart/ that God, by whose grace alone I am what I am,[3] is praised in my art;/ but I also fear to appear to be more than what I am. I am convinced that both would be wrong: to deny God's gracious gift to one;/ and to pretend to have received a gift when one has received none./

---

1   Some of the "learned men" may have been Gerberga's former teachers at Saint Emmeram (Winterfeld, *Opera*, p. iii); Archbishop Bruno of Cologne is almost certain to have been one of them (Dronke, *Women Writers*, p. 57).

2   Reference is to Deuteronomy 19:15.

3   Reference is to I Corinthians 15:10. As Dronke, *Women Writers*, p. 74, observes, her audience "will have recognized her Pauline citation and been aware of its context – a mingled pride and humility close to Hrotsvitha's Paul passes from 'I am the least of the Apostles, I who am not worthy to be called an apostle' to 'but I laboured more abundantly than all the apostles – not I, however, but the grace of God with me.' "

I do not deny that by the gift of the Creator's grace I am able to grasp certain concepts the arts concerning/ because I am a creature capable of learning,/ but I also know that through my own powers, I know nothing./ I also know that God gave me a sharp mind, but my mind has remained/ neglected through my own inertia and untrained/ ever since the efforts of my teachers ceased to nurture it. Therefore, in order to prevent God's gift in me from dying by my neglect, I have tried whenever I could probe,/ to rip small patches from Philosophy's robe/ and weave them into this little work of mine,/ so that the worthlessness of my own ignorance may be ennobled by their interweaving of this nobler material's shine,/ and that, thus, the Giver of my talent all the more justly be praised through me,/ the more limited the female intellect is believed to be./ This alone was my intention in writing, my only thought;/ this alone was the reason why my work was wrought/. I do not boast to possess knowledge nor do I pretend not to be ignorant; but, as far as I am concerned, the only thing I know is that I know naught./ But touched by your good will and your encouragement, in the manner of the reed by the breeze,/[4] I was encouraged, I was put at ease/ to send you this little book for examination/ which I have written with such an intention/ but have preferred to keep hidden until now rather than show it openly because of its worthlessness./ It behooves you to examine and correct it with no slight carefulness/ as if it were the fruit of your own labor. And then, righted according to the rules of correct composition,/ send it back to me, so that, enlightened by your instruction/ I may be able to recognize where I have failed the most.

---

4   Reference is to Matthew 11:7.

The Martyrdom of the Holy Virgins
Agape, Chionia, and Hirena

(Dulcitius)[1]

The martyrdom of the holy virgins Agape, Chionia and Hirena whom, in the silence of the night, Governor Dulcitius secretly visited, desiring to delight in their embrace. But as soon as he entered,/ he became demented/ and kissed and hugged the pots and pans, mistaking them for the girls until his face and his clothes were soiled with disgusting black dirt. Afterward Count Sissinus, acting on orders,/ was given the girls so he might put them to tortures./ He, too, was deluded miraculously/ but finally ordered that Agape and Chionia be burnt and Hirena be slain by an arrow./[2]

*

Diocletian:	The renown of your free and noble descent/ and the brightness of your beauty demand/ that you be <u>married</u> to one of the foremost men of my court. This will be done according to our command if you deny Christ and comply by bringing offerings to our gods.
Agape:	Be free of care,/ don't trouble yourself to prepare our wedding/ because we cannot be compelled under any duress/ to betray Christ's holy name, which we must confess,/ nor to stain our virginity.
Diocletian:	What madness possesses you? What rage drives you three?/
Agape:	What signs of our madness do you see?/
Diocletian:	An obvious and great display./
Agape:	In what way?/

---

1 Cf. the legend in *Acta Sanctorum*, April 1. My translation of *Dulcitius* first appeared in *Medieval Women Writers* (Athens: University of Georgia Press, 1984). It is reprinted here with the kind permission of the University of Georgia Press. On the humor of the play, see Sandro Sticca, "Sacred Drama and Comic Realism in the Plays of Hrotsvitha of Gandersheim," in *Acta VI. The Middle Ages*, ed. William Snyder (Binghamton, 1979), pp. 117–43. *Dulcitius, Calimachus, Abraham*, and *Sapientia* first appeared in K. M. Wilson, *The Plays of Hrotsvit of Gandersheim* (New York: Garland, 1988 (now out of print)).

2 The martyrdom of the three virgins occurred during Diocletian's persecution of the Christians in Thessalonica in 290. The girls' names denote Love, Purity and Peace.

Diocletian:	Chiefly in that renouncing the practices of ancient religion/ you follow the useless, new-fangled ways of the Christian superstition./[3]
Agape:	Heedlessly you offend the majesty of the omnipotent God. That is dangerous . . .[4]
Diocletian:	Dangerous to whom?
Agape:	To you and to the state you rule./
Diocletian:	She is mad; remove the fool!/
Chionia:	My sister is not mad; she rightly reprehended your folly.
Diocletian:	She rages even more madly; remove her from our sight and arraign the third girl./
Hirena:	You will find the third, too, a rebel/ and resisting you forever./
Diocletian:	Hirena, although you are younger in birth,/ be greater in worth!/
Hirena:	Show me, I pray, how?
Diocletian:	Bow your neck to the gods, set an example for your sisters, and be the cause for their freedom!
Hirena:	Let those worship idols, Sire,/ who wish to incur God's ire./ But I won't defile my head, anointed with royal unguent by debasing myself at the idols' feet.
Diocletian:	The worship of gods brings no dishonor/ but great honor./
Hirena:	And what dishonor is more disgraceful,/ what disgrace is any more shameful/ than when a slave is venerated as a master?
Diocletian:	I don't ask you to worship slaves/ but the mighty gods of princes and greats./
Hirena:	Is he not anyone's slave/ who, for a price, is up for sale?/
Diocletian:	For her speech so brazen,/ to the tortures she must be taken./
Hirena:	This is just what we hope for, this is what we desire,/ that for the love of Christ through tortures we may expire./
Diocletian:	Let these insolent girls/ who defy our decrees and words/ be put in chains and kept in the squalor of prison until Governor Dulcitius can examine them.

*

---

[3] As Christians accused the pagan Romans of superstition, so did the Romans accuse the Christians of the same.

[4] An example of Hrotsvit's use of aposeopesis.

Dulcitius:	Bring forth, soldiers, the girls whom you hold sequestered./
Soldiers:	Here they are whom you requested./
Dulcitius:	Wonderful, indeed, how beautiful, how graceful, how admirable these little girls are!
Soldiers:	Yes, they are perfectly lovely.
Dulcitius:	I am captivated by their beauty.
Soldiers:	That is understandable.
Dulcitius:	To draw them to my heart, I am eager./
Soldiers:	Your success will be meager./
Dulcitius:	Why?
Soldiers:	Because they are firm in faith.
Dulcitius:	What if I sway them by flattery?/
Soldiers:	They will despise it utterly./
Dulcitius:	What if with tortures I frighten them?/
Soldiers:	Little will it matter to them./
Dulcitius:	Then what should be done, I wonder?/
Soldiers:	Carefully you should ponder./
Dulcitius:	Place them under guard in the inner room of the pantry, where they keep the servants' pots./[5]
Soldiers:	Why in that particular spot?/
Dulcitius:	So that I may visit them often at my leisure./
Soldiers:	At your pleasure./
Dulcitius:	What do the captives do at this time of night?/
Soldiers:	Hymns they recite./
Dulcitius:	Let us go near./
Soldiers:	From afar we hear their tinkling little voices clear./
Dulcitius:	Stand guard before the door with your lantern/ but I will enter/ and satisfy myself in their longed-for embrace./
Soldiers:	Enter. We will guard this place./

*

Agape:	What is that noise outside the door?/
Hirena:	That wretched Dulcitius coming to the fore./
Chionia:	May God protect us!
Agape:	Amen.
Chionia:	What is the meaning of this clash of the pots and the pans?
Hirena:	I will check./ Come here, please, and look through the crack!/
Agape:	What is going on?

---

5 For an excellent discussion of the medieval significance of kitchens and pots and pans, see Sandro Sticca, "Hrotswith's *Dulcitius* and Christian Symbolism," pp. 108–27.

Hirena:	Look, the fool, the madman base,/ he thinks he is enjoying our embrace./
Agape:	What is he doing?
Hirena:	Into his lap he pulls the utensils,/ he embraces the pots and the pans, giving them tender kisses./
Chionia:	Ridiculous!
Hirena:	His face, his hands, his clothes, are so soiled, so filthy, that with all the soot that clings to him, he looks like an Ethiopian.[6]
Agape:	It is only right that he should appear in body the way he is in his mind: possessed by the Devil.
Hirena:	Wait! He prepares to leave. Let us watch how he is greeted,/ and how he is treated/ by the soldiers who wait for him.

*

Soldiers:	Who is coming out?/ A demon without doubt./ Or rather, the Devil himself is he;/ let us flee!/
Dulcitius:	Soldiers, where are you taking yourselves in flight?/ Stay! Wait! Escort me home with your light!/
Soldiers:	The voice is our master's tone/ but the look the Devil's own./ Let us not stay!/ Let us run away; the apparition will slay us!/
Dulcitius:	I will go to the palace and complain,/ and reveal to the whole court the insults I had to sustain./

*

Dulcitius:	Guards, let me into the palace;/ I must have a private audience./
Guards:	Who is this vile and detestable monster covered in torn and despicable rags? Let us beat him,/ from the steps let us sweep him;/ he must not be allowed to enter.
Dulcitius:	Alas, alas, what has happened? Am I not dressed in splendid garments? Don't I look neat and clean?/ Yet anyone who looks at my mien/ loathes me as a foul monster. To my wife I shall return,/ and from her learn/ what has happened. But there is my spouse,/ with disheveled hair she leaves the house,/ and the whole household follows her in tears.

---

6   Sticca, *ibid.*, pp. 112ff, discusses the symbolic function of the play by emphasizing the figurative meaning of the Dulcitius-Devil-Cook analogy, and by showing that in the play the kitchen is the symbolical infernal portrait of Hell, where Dulcitius's moral corruption is accomplished, and that the pots and pans he embraces are the processes of that corruption.

*

Wife:	Alas, alas, my Lord Dulcitius, what has happened to you?/ You are not sane; the Christians have made a laughing stock out of you./
Dulcitius:	Now I know at last. I owe this mockery to their witchcraft.[7]
Wife:	What upsets me so, what makes me more sad, is that you were ignorant of all that happened to you.
Dulcitius:	I command that those insolent girls be led forth,/ and that they be publicly stripped of all their clothes,/ so that they experience similar mockery in retaliation for ours.
Soldiers:	We labor in vain;/ we sweat without gain./Behold, their garments stick to their virginal bodies like skin,/ and he who urged us to strip them snores in his seat,/ and he cannot be awakened from his sleep./ Let us go to the Emperor and report what has happened.

*

Diocletian:	It grieves me very much/ to hear that Governor Dulcitius has been so greatly deluded,/ so greatly insulted,/ so utterly humiliated./ But these vile young women shall not boast with impunity of having made a mockery of our gods and those who worship them. I shall direct Count Sissinus to take due vengeance.

*

Sissinus:	Soldiers, where are those insolent girls who are to be tortured?
Soldiers:	They are kept in prison.
Sissinus:	Leave Hirena there,/ bring the others here./
Soldiers:	Why do you except the one?
Sissinus:	Sparing her youth. Perchance, she may be converted easier, if she is not intimidated by her sisters' presence./
Soldiers:	That makes sense./

---

[7] Hrotsvit's term (to be repeated later) is *maleficia*, the beneficent sorcery of God. Peter Dronke, *Women Writers*, p. 61, points out that "the illusions that seem 'malefic' to the pagans are in fact innocent, and always in the comic mode."

*

Soldiers:	Here are the girls whose presence you requested.
Sissinus:	Agape and Chionia, give heed,/ and to my council accede!/
Agape:	We will not give heed./
Sissinus:	Bring offerings to the gods.
Agape:	We bring offerings of praise forever/ to the true Father eternal,/ and to His Son co-eternal,/ and also to the Holy Spirit.
Sissinus:	This is not what I bid,/ but on pain of penalty prohibit./
Agape:	You cannot prohibit it; neither shall we ever sacrifice to demons.
Sissinus:	Cease this hardness of heart, and make your offerings. But if you persist,/ then I shall insist/ that you be killed according to the Emperor's orders.
Chionia:	It is only proper that you should obey the orders of your Emperor, whose decrees we disdain, as you know. For if you wait and try to spare us, then you could be rightfully killed.
Sissinus:	Soldiers, do not delay,/ take these blaspheming girls away,/ and throw them alive into the flames.
Soldiers:	We shall instantly build the pyre you asked for, and we will cast these girls into the raging fire, and thus we'll put an end to these insults at last./
Agape:	O Lord, nothing is impossible for Thee;/ even the fire forgets its nature and obeys Thee;/ but we are weary of delay;/ therefore, dissolve the earthly bonds that hold our souls, we pray,/ so that as our earthly bodies die,/ our souls my sing your praise in Heaven.
Soldiers:	Oh, marvel, oh stupendous miracle! Behold their souls are no longer bound to their bodies,/ yet no traces of injury can be found; neither their hair, nor their clothes are burnt by the fire,/ and their bodies are not at all harmed by the pyre./
Sissinus:	Bring forth Hirena.

*

Soldiers:	Here she is.
Sissinus:	Hirena, tremble at the deaths of your sisters and fear to perish according to their example.
Hirena:	I hope to follow their example and expire,/ so with them in Heaven eternal joy I may acquire./
Sissinus:	Give in, give in to my persuasion./

(handwritten margin notes: "Power of three"; "Phoenix / allegory.")

Hirena:	I will never yield to evil persuasion./
Sissinus:	If you don't yield, I shall not give you a quick and easy death, but multiply your sufferings.
Hirena:	The more cruelly I'll be tortured,/ the more gloriously I'll be exalted./
Sissinus:	You fear no tortures, no pain?/ What you abhor, I shall ordain./
Hirena:	Whatever punishment you design,/ I will escape with help Divine./
Sissinus:	To a brothel you will be consigned,/ where your body will be shamefully defiled./
Hirena:	It is better that the body be dirtied with any stain than that the soul be polluted with idolatry.
Sissinus:	If you are so polluted in the company of harlots, you can no longer be counted among the virginal choir.
Hirena:	Lust deserves punishment, but forced compliance the crown. With neither is one considered guilty,/ unless the soul consents freely./
Sissinus:	In vain have I spared her, in vain have I pitied her youth.
Soldiers:	We knew this before;/ for on no possible score/ can she be moved to adore our gods, nor can she be broken by terror.
Sissinus:	I shall spare her no longer./
Soldiers:	Rightly you ponder./
Sissinus:	Seize her without mercy,/ drag her with cruelty,/ and take her in dishonor to the brothel./
Hirena:	They will not do it./
Sissinus:	Who can prohibit it?/
Hirena:	He whose foresight rules the world./
Sissinus:	I shall see . . ./
Hirena:	Sooner than you wish, it will be./
Sissinus:	Soldiers, be not afraid/ of what this blaspheming girl has said./
Soldiers:	We are not afraid,/ but eagerly follow what you bade./

*

Sissinus:	Who are those approaching? How similar they are to the men/ to whom we gave Hirena just then./ They are the same. Why are you returning so fast?/ Why so out of breath, I ask?/
Soldiers:	You are the one for whom we look./
Sissinus:	Where is she whom you just took?/

Soldiers:	On the peak of the mountain.
Sissinus:	Which one?
Soldiers:	The one close by.
Sissinus:	Oh you idiots, dull and blind./ You have completely lost your mind!/
Soldiers:	Why do you accuse us,/ why do you abuse us,/why do you threaten us with menacing voice and face?
Sissinus:	May the gods destroy you!
Soldiers:	What have we committed? What harm have we done? How have we transgressed against your orders?
Sissinus:	Have I not given the orders that you should take that rebel against the gods to a brothel?
Soldiers:	Yes, so you did command,/ and we were eager to fulfill your demand,/ but two strangers intercepted us/ saying that you sent them to us/ to lead Hirena to the mountain's peak.
Sissinus:	That's new to me./
Soldiers:	We can see./
Sissinus:	What were they like?/
Soldiers:	Splendidly dressed and an awe-inspiring sight./
Sissinus:	Did you follow?/
Soldiers:	We did so./
Sissinus:	What did they do?/
Soldiers:	They placed themselves on Hirena's left and right,/ and told us to be forthright/ and not to hide from you what happened.
Sissinus:	I see a sole recourse,/ that I should mount my horse/ and seek out those who so freely made sport with us.

*

Sissinus:	Hmm, I don't know what to do. I am bewildered by the witchcraft of these Christians. I keep going around the mountain and keep finding this track/ but I neither know how to proceed nor how to find my way back./
Soldiers:	We are all deluded by some intrigue;/ we are afflicted with a great fatigue;/ if you allow this insane person to stay alive,/ then neither you nor we shall survive./
Sissinus:	Anyone among you,/ I don't care which,/ string a bow, and shoot an arrow, and kill that witch!/
Soldiers:	Rightly so./
Hirena:	Wretched Sissinus, blush for shame, and proclaim your miserable defeat because without the help of weapons, you cannot overcome a tender little virgin as your foe./

Sissinus: Whatever the shame that may be mine, I will bear it more easily now because I know for certain that you will die.

Hirena: This is the greatest joy I can conceive,/ but for you this is a cause to grieve,/ because you shall be damned in Tartarus for your cruelty,/ while I shall receive the martyr's palm and the crown of virginity;/ thus I will enter the heavenly bridal chamber of the Eternal King, to whom are all honor and glory in all eternity./

virgin symbolism — Artemis & doe
reference to the "hunt"
arrow shoot

The Resurrection of Drusiana and Calimachus

(Calimachus)[1]

The resurrection of Drusiana and Calimachus, who loved her not only while she was alive, but driven by despair and the abominable curse of illicit lust,/ he loved her more than is just/ even after she died in the Lord./ Therefore he suffered his just reward/ and died, bitten by a snake./ However, for Saint John the Apostle's prayers' sake,/ together with Drusiana, he was resurrected and was born again in Christ.[2]

*

Calimachus:	My friends, I'd like to have a few words with you.
Friends:	We are at your disposal.
Calimachus:	If you don't mind, I'd take you aside, away from the others.
Friends:	Whatever pleases you is fine with us.
Calimachus:	Let's find a more private location,/ so that passers-by will not interrupt our conversation./
Friends:	As you like.
Calimachus:	For long I have suffered a painful affliction./ By your council I hope to improve my condition./
Friends:	It is only right/ that we share like and like/ whatever happens to any one of us in total sympathy,/ whether it be good luck or misery./
Calimachus:	Oh, if you could only take part/ and share my pain with a compassionate heart!/
Friends:	Tell us why you suffer; and if it warrants sympathy, we shall sympathize; if not, we shall try to dissuade you from an unworthy deed.[3]

---

1 Hrotsvit's source, the apocryphal Acts of John, was severely criticized by the Council of Nicaea, because of its Manichean tendencies. See Homeyer, *Opera*, pp. 278–79.

2 Because of the tomb-scene and other correspondences, *Calimachus* has been compared to Shakespeare's *Romeo and Juliet*. See Paul von Winterfeld, *Deutsche Dichter*, p. 105.

3 Note that Calimachus's friends already anticipate the possibility of immoral action.

Calimachus:	I love!
Friends:	What?
Calimachus:	Something comely,/ something lovely./
Friends:	That applies neither to one in specific nor to all in general; thus whatever you love cannot be understood by that description at all./
Calimachus:	It is a woman!
Friends:	When you say a woman, you refer to all./
Calimachus:	No, not to all equally,/ but to one specifically./
Friends:	What one says about a particular subject is of no help unless it differentiates it from other entities./ Therefore, if you want us to know this particular, give us its essential qualities./[4]
Calimachus:	I love Drusiana.
Friends:	Lord Andronicus's wife?
Calimachus:	Yes.
Friends:	Friend, be advised;/ you are making a mistake – she is baptized./
Calimachus:	That's of no concern to me/ as long as I can make her fall in love with me./
Friends:	You will fail./
Calimachus:	Why do you doubt that I will prevail?/
Friends:	Because you attempt a difficult task./
Calimachus:	I am not the first to attempt such a task,/ and am I not encouraged to dare to try it, I ask/ by the example of many?[5]
Friends:	Listen to us, brother: she for whom you burn in passion/ follows Saint John the Apostle's instruction/ and has devoted herself entirely to God, so much so that she doesn't even visit the bed of Andronicus who is a Christian. How much less likely is she/ to give in to your vain carnality?/[6]
Calimachus:	I have sought your consolation,/ but you drive me to desperation./
Friends:	He who pretends, deceives; and he who flatters, sells truth.
Calimachus:	Since you refuse me your help, I'll go to her myself and try to seduce her with flattery./

---

[4] This differentiation of categories is mentioned, among others, by Boethius, *Inst. Arithm.* I, 1.

[5] As a pagan, Calimachus refers to the gods' love-affairs as well as human precedents.

[6] Apparently, Drusiana and Andronicus are now living in a synesaictical (i.e. in the past consummated but now chaste) marriage.

Friends:	You will fail entirely./
Calimachus:	I shall go even if the fates oppose me./
Friends:	We shall see./

*

Calimachus:	I would like to speak with you, Drusiana, love of my heart.
Drusiana:	Why should you wish to speak with me Calimachus, I wonder?/
Calimachus:	You wonder?/
Drusiana:	Yes.
Calimachus:	First, I'd like to speak of love./
Drusiana:	Of what love?/
Calimachus:	The love I feel for you above all others.
Drusiana:	What bond of kinship,/ what legal relationship/ compels you to love me?[7]
Calimachus:	Your beauty does./
Drusiana:	My beauty does?/
Calimachus:	Yes, that is true./
Drusiana:	What is my beauty to you?/
Calimachus:	Alas, very little so far, but I hope to gain much more in the future.
Drusiana:	Out of my sight, out of my sight, you vile seducer; I blush to speak with you for even a short while, for I perceive you to be full of diabolical guile.
Calimachus:	My Drusiana, do not repel him who loves you,/ who with the passion of all his heart adores you/ but return my love!
Drusiana:	I'm not in the least touched by your seductive art;/ I abhor your lust and despise you with all my heart./
Calimachus:	So far I have no reason to get angry or mad,/ because the reaction which my love elicited in you could very well make you turn red./
Drusiana:	I feel no reaction except for disgust./
Calimachus:	But you will change your mind, I trust./
Drusiana:	I will never change my mind on this matter./

---

7   Hrotsvit's dialogue here relies on deliberate misunderstandings. The rhymed (homoeoteleuton) stychomythia reinforces the dialogue's irony. As Sandro Sticco observed in "Sacred Drama and Comic Realism in the Plays of Hrotsvitha of Gandersheim," in *Acta VI. The Early Middle Ages*, ed. William Snyder (Binghamton, 1979), p. 132, this passage reveals a type of humor whereby "... particularly in scenes of love, the comic element arises out the absurdity of the situation as the pagan lovers are shown to be spasmodically incongruous under the influence of their passion."

Calimachus:	Perhaps you will – and for the better./
Drusiana:	You insane fool, why do you deceive yourself? Why do you delude yourself with an empty dream?/ By what token, through what insanity extreme,/ do you believe that I would ever yield to your frivolity's crime,/ I who have abstained from visiting the bed even of my lawfully wedded husband for a long time./
Calimachus:	By God I swear: if you don't yield to me, I will not rest,/ I will not desist from pursuing my quest/ until I entrap you with clever guiles.

*

Drusiana:	Alas, my Lord Jesus Christ, what is the good of the vow of chastity I swore/ if this madman is crazed on my beauty's score?/ Oh, Lord, look upon my fear,/ look upon the pain I bear!/ I don't know what to do; if I denounce him, there will be public scandal on my account, I'm afraid;/ if I keep it secret, I cannot avoid falling into these devilish snares without Thy aid./ Help me, O Christ, therefore, with my plan/ and permit me to die so that I won't become the ruin of that charming young man./
Andronicus:	Woe is me, unhappy man!/ Drusiana is suddenly dead. I must hurry and call Saint John.
John:	Andronicus, why so void of cheers,/ why this torrent of tears?/
Andronicus:	Alas, my Lord, I am weary of my life./
John:	What happened to you, what strife?/
Andronicus:	Drusiana, your disciple . . .
John:	Did she expire?/
Andronicus:	Yes.
John:	It is very inappropriate to shed tears for those who decease/ but whose souls we believe to be enjoying eternal peace./
Andronicus:	I have no doubt that her soul enjoys eternal peace, as you say, and that her body will one day be resurrected./ Yet I am much pained and distracted/ that in my very presence she begged for death to take her.
John:	Do you know the cause? What is your belief?/
Andronicus:	I know it and I will tell you when I have recovered from my grief./
John:	Let us go ahead/ and celebrate the service for the dead./
Andronicus:	There is a marble tomb nearby./ There her body shall lie./

	The care for guarding the tomb shall be entrusted to Fortunatus, my overseer.[8]
John:	It is proper that she be buried with all honor. May God give her soul joy and eternal rest.

*

Calimachus:	Fortunatus, what will happen? I cannot renounce my love even after Drusiana has died.
Fortunatus:	Most unfortunate!
Calimachus:	I shall die unless you are willing to help./
Fortunatus:	How can I be of help?/
Calimachus:	In that you let me see the dead.
Fortunatus:	She has remained unharmed because no long sickness wasted her body away, but a mild fever killed her.
Calimachus:	I would have been happy had I never heard.
Fortunatus:	If you pay me well, you shall have her body to use as you wish.
Calimachus:	Take in the meantime what I have on me. Don't worry; later I'll give you more./
Fortunatus:	Let's go right away./
Calimachus:	I certainly won't delay./
Fortunatus:	Here is the body. The face is not disintegrated,/ and her limbs are not yet wasted./ Use it as you please!
Calimachus:	O, Drusiana, Drusiana, how I loved you with all my heart's fire,/ with what sincere affection I was bound to you, and yet you kept rejecting me and kept opposing my desire./ Now it is within my power to inflict any injury I wish upon you, my dear./
Fortunatus:	Ah, a frightful snake draws near!/
Calimachus:	Woe is me, Fortunatus, why did you deceive me? Why did you persuade me to do this detestable deed? Now you die bitten by the serpent and I die with you out of fear./

*

John:	Let us go, Andronicus, to Drusiana's grave/ so that we may commend her soul to Christ in prayer.
Andronicus:	It behooves your holiness not to forget those who placed their trust in you.

---

8   Fortunatus's name already hints at his avaricious character.

John:	Behold the invisible God appears visible in the likeness of a handsome young man.
Andronicus:	I tremble.
John:	Christ, Our Lord, why dost Thou deign to appear/ and manifest Thyself to Thy servants here?/
God:	I have come to resurrect Drusiana and the youth who lies next to her grave, because my name is to be glorified in them.
Andronicus:	How suddenly He disappeared from sight!
John:	I still don't understand the reason for this.
Andronicus:	Let us hurry. Perhaps you will understand when we arrive there what you don't understand now.

*

John:	In Christ's name, what marvel is this I see? Behold, Drusiana's body lies in the foreground;/ next to her lie two dead bodies in a serpent's coil bound./
Andronicus:	I suspect what this might mean. This here is Calimachus, who loved Drusiana illicitly with forbidden passion; this was the reason why she, ill with sorrow, caught a fever/ and prayed that death might take her./
John:	Her love of chastity forced her to act so.
Andronicus:	After her death, this madman was consumed by the languish of his unhappy desire/ and the disappointment of his thwarted crime increased the flames of his passion's fire./
John:	Miserable wretch!
Andronicus:	I don't have any doubts that he bribed this wicked slave so that he might have an occasion to perform an abominable and grave deed./
John:	O, incomparable sacrilege!
Andronicus:	That's the reason, as I see, why both were killed – so that the atrocious deed could not be carried out./
John:	And rightly so, without a doubt./
Andronicus:	In all this, what surprises me most is that the Divine Voice announced the resurrection of him who willed such an evil deed, rather than of the other who simply consented to be an accomplice for hire, unless perhaps it was because this man had sinned, blinded by carnal desire,/ and so out of ignorance,/while the other sinned out of malice./
John:	With what exact discernment the Supreme Judge weighs all that is done, and how equitably He balances the merits

of every one, is not obvious to man nor can it be easily explained/ because the subtlety of the Divine Judge far surpasses the capacity of the human brain./

Andronicus: Therefore we fail to understand and continue to wonder/ because we fail to grasp the reasons why things happen, regardless of how intently we ponder./

John: Often an occurrence after the deed teaches us the reasons for the initial decision.

Andronicus: So, blessed John, do what you must do; be resolved/ and resurrect Calimachus so that the knot of this mystery may be solved./

John: First, in the name of Christ, the snake must be ejected,/ and then only should Calimachus be resurrected./

Andronicus: Your thinking is wise;/ this way Calimachus will not be bitten again and may rise./

John: Away from hence, you cursed beast.

Andronicus: It heard what you ordered and obeyed right away.

John: Christ's power, not my own, worked this feat./

Andronicus: Therefore the beast fled before you finished to speak./

John: O God, scrutable and incomprehensible,/ simple and inestimable,/ Thou alone art what Thou art. Mixing two diverse elements, Thou created man; separating the same two elements, Thou dissolved what made up the whole./ Grant that Calimachus rise up, his breath returned, and the disjointed elements may be joined again as a whole,/ just as he was as a man, so Thou mayst be glorified by all,/ Thou, who alone worked this miracle.

Andronicus: Amen. Behold he is breathing again,/ but is stunned and motionless must remain./

John: Calimachus, rise in Christ's name and confess all that has happened. Tell us, however vile the vice,/ so that nothing is hidden; only the full truth will suffice./

Calimachus: I cannot deny that I came to perpetrate a deed heinous and dire/ because I was consumed by an unhappy desire,/ and I could not subdue the fervor of my forbidden passion.

John: What madness, what craze held you in chains/ that you would presume to inflict the injury of dishonor upon these chaste remains?/

Calimachus: My own madness and Fortunatus's fraudulent guile.

John: Were you, thrice miserable wretch, unfortunate enough to perpetrate this vile sacrilege as planned?

Calimachus:	No, as a matter of fact./ I didn't lack the will but lacked the opportunity to act./
John:	What prevented you?
Calimachus:	When I first removed the shroud and attempted to harm the lifeless corpse with insults, this Fortunatus, the kindler of my evil, the inspiration of my sin, died, poisoned by the snake's venom.
John:	O, well done!
Calimachus:	But to me a youth appeared, of terrifying sight/ who respectfully covered the naked corpse as He did alight./ From His flaming countenance sparks rained on the place/ and one of them, rebounding, hit my face./ At the same time I heard a voice that cried:/ "Calimachus, die so that you may live." Then I died./
John:	It was the working of Heavenly Grace, that never rejoices in the perdition of sinners.
Calimachus:	You heard the misery of my perdition; do not put off dispersing your pity's gift./
John:	I will not put it off. I will be swift./
Calimachus:	For I am ashamed; my heart is pained by grief./ I mourn, and I grieve; I suffer because of the enormity of my sin.
John:	And not unjustly, for such a grave offense/ will require no slight penitence./
Calimachus:	O, if I could only open the secret door/ of my inmost heart and soul,/ so that you could see the bitter anguish of my suffering, and take pity on the patient's woe./
John:	I rejoice in your grief because your sadness will help heal you, I know./
Calimachus:	I abhor my former life. I abhor my sinful lust./
John:	And so you must./
Calimachus:	That I have sinned, I rue./
John:	Rightly you do./
Calimachus:	All that I have done, I now despise and find appalling/ – so much so that no love, no desire for life I find now enthralling/ unless, reborn in Christ, I may merit to be transformed into a better man.
John:	I have no doubts that Supreme Grace will make itself manifest in you.
Calimachus:	Therefore do not delay, do not wait to raise up the fallen, to bring consolation to the grieving so that by your admonition/ and under your tuition/ I may be transformed from a pagan into a Christian: from a worthless man/ into a

	chaste and virtuous man/ and that under your guidance I may walk the straight path of verity/ and may live according to the proclaimed promises of Divine Charity./
John:	Praise be to the only begotten Son of God, partaker in our human frailty who killed you, Calimachus, my son, in order to spare you and gave you life by making you die, so that by this apparent death He might liberate your soul from eternal damnation./
Andronicus:	A miraculous event, worthy of all admiration./
John:	O Christ, the world's redeemer, Thou who suffered for us sinners, I know not how to praise Thee,/ how to glorify Thee:/ I am overcome by Thy kind mercy and Thy merciful patience. Like a father Thou toleratest the misdoings of sinners at times,/ and at other times Thou forcest them with just reproach to repent of their crimes./
Andronicus:	Divine Mercy be praised!
John:	Who would have dared to believe/ and who would have presumed the hope to conceive/ that this man, whom, tainted with vile sin, death had found and taken/ Thy mercy would reawaken,/ and that he would be found worthy to find forgiveness. Blessed be Thy name in all eternity, Thou who alone can perform such stupendous miracles.
Andronicus:	Now Saint John, do not tarry in consoling me; please heed my request,/ for the love of my wife Drusiana will not let me rest/ until I see her resurrected too./
John:	Drusiana, may our Lord Jesus Christ resurrect you!/
Drusiana:	Praise be to thee, O Christ, for reviving me.
Calimachus:	Thanks be to the Savior who gave you new life in joy, my Drusiana, after you have died in grave and extreme sadness.
Drusiana:	It would suit your saintliness, reverend father John, that after reviving Calimachus, who loved me unlawfully, you would also revive the one who proved himself a traitor to my tomb.
Calimachus:	Apostle of Christ, do not deem that traitor, that evildoer, worthy of regaining his breath/ of absolving him from the chains of death,/ him who deceived me, who seduced me, who prompted me to attempt that horrible deed!/
John:	You should not envy him that, by Divine Grace, he too may be freed./
Calimachus:	But he is not worthy of resurrection/ who is the author of another's perdition./

John:	The law of our religion teaches us to forgive those who trespass against us if we hope that God forgives us our trespasses against Him – and so we must./
Andronicus:	And so it is just./
John:	When God's only begotten Son, firstborn of the Virgin who alone is without sin, who alone is pure, and who alone came into the world without original sin's stain,/ found all of us men weighed down with sin's heavy burden and pain./
Andronicus:	That is true and plain./
John:	So, even though He found not one man of righteous ways,/ not one worthy of grace,/ He did not spurn anyone, did not deprive anyone of His mercy's grace, but He gave Himself and His precious blood for all of us.
Andronicus:	Had the innocent Lamb not been killed,/ no one would have been freed./
John:	Therefore He takes no delight in the perdition of men whom He redeemed with His precious blood./
Andronicus:	Thanks be to God!/
John:	Therefore we should never envy/ others the gift of God's mercy,/ which we enjoy in abundance/ without ever having merited it once./
Calimachus:	Your admonition frightens me./
John:	But so that I don't appear to go against your plea,/ he will not be revived by me/ but by Drusiana, because God gave her the grace to do this.
Drusiana:	O Divine Substance, who alone art truly without material form, Thou who hast made me in Thy own image and breathed life into Thy creation, grant that warmth may return to Fortunatus's earthly form so that he may become a living being once again, and that our triple resurrection may be turned into the praise of the Venerable Trinity!
John:	Amen.
Drusiana:	Fortunatus, rise up and by Christ's command throw off the chains of death!/
Fortunatus:	Whose hand raised me? Whose voice revived me? Who returned my breath?/
John:	Drusiana.
Fortunatus:	Drusiana revived me?/
John:	Yes, it was she./
Fortunatus:	Did she not die several days ago suddenly?/
John:	Yes, but she lives in Christ.

Fortunatus:	And why is Calimachus standing there, modest and with a serious face,/ not raving, like before, for the love of Drusiana's embrace?/
John:	Because, converted from evil intent,/ he is now truly bent/ to be Christ's disciple.
Fortunatus:	Oh, no!/
John:	Oh yes, it is so./
Fortunatus:	If, as you say, Drusiana revived me and Calimachus is converted, then I renounce life and freely elect to die, for I would rather be dead/ than see such an abundant spread/ of the power of grace in them.
John:	O wondrous envy of Satan; O, malice of the ancient snake who gave death to our first parents and always moans over the victory of the just!/ This most unfortunate Fortunatus, full of Satan's bitter fall, I trust/ is like an evil shoot producing bitter fruit. Therefore, cut off from the community of the faithful and ejected from the flock of God-fearing men, he should be condemned to eternal fire's pain,/ tormented without any hope for coolness again./[9]
Andronicus:	Behold, suddenly he is bloated where the serpent bit him, and he is dead/ quicker than it can be said./
John:	Let him die; let him be Hell's denizen,/ he who out of envy of another's merits refused to be earth's citizen./
Andronicus:	How awful!
John:	Nothing is more horrifying than envy, nothing more sinful than pride.
Andronicus:	Both are dreadful.
John:	Both sins act in one and the same man because neither can be without the other: together they are bound./
Andronicus:	Why? Please, expound./
John:	It is because he who is proud, is envious, and he who is envious, is proud, for the envious mind cannot bear to hear anyone else's praise and will try to denigrate those who in comparison with him are deemed better. He will never condescend to submit to his betters/ and in his pride he will try to rise above his equals in all matters./
Andronicus:	That seems clear.
John:	That is why this miserable wretch was afflicted in his mind; because he could not bear to find himself inferior

---

9   Cf. Matthew, 7:17.

	to these two/ in whom he perceived God's grace shining through./
Andronicus:	Now I grasp it, it's finally plain:/ he was not enumerated among the resurrected, because he was to die immediately again./
John:	He was deserving of both deaths because first he injured the tomb entrusted to his keep/ and second, he attacked the resurrected with a hatred unjust and deep./
Andronicus:	The wretch is now dead.
John:	Let us return and not stay any further, let us leave the Devil's son to his father. But we should spend this day of Calimachus's conversion and the resurrection of both Calimachus and Drusiana in rejoicing. Let us give thanks to God, the equitable Judge who knows our secrets' inmost recesses,/ and who alone assesses/ everything with care/ and who in weighing all things is always fair,/ allotting to everyone according to his merits, his deserved gain or punishment. To Him be all honor and glory,/ strength and victory,/ praise and jubilation from eternity to eternity,/ for now and forever. Amen.

The Fall and Repentance of Mary

(Abraham)[1]

The fall and repentance of Mary, the hermit Abraham's niece,/ who, after she had lived twenty years in anchoritic peace/ and had lost her virginity,/ returned to the world's vanity,/ and did not even fear to live in a brothel with prostitutes. But after two years, admonished by the aforementioned Abraham, who sought her out disguised as a lover, she returned and purged herself from the stains of her sins for a period twenty years lasting,/ through effusive tears, vigils, prayers and the constant exercise of fasting./[2]

*

Abraham:	Do you, brother and cohermit Effrem, find it convenient to speak with me now, or do you wish for me to wait until you have finished your divine prayer?
Effrem:	Our conversation should always be in His praise, who promised to be in the midst of those who have gathered in His name.
Abraham:	I have come to speak of nothing else except of what I know is in concordance with God's will.
Effrem:	Then I shall not keep myself from you another moment, but give myself entirely to your concern.
Abraham:	A certain impending task has upset my mind/ concerning which I hope that you will be inclined/to concur with my judgment.
Effrem:	As we are to be of one heart and one soul, we ought to have the same likes/ and also the same dislikes./
Abraham:	I have a young niece bereaved of the solace of both

1 *Abraham* is based on a legend ascribed to the Syrian Ephrem (fourth century); Hrotsvit's source, the Latin translation of the *vita*, originated in the sixth century. Cf. Homeyer, *Opera*, pp. 288–302.

2 Cf. *Acta Sanctorum*, March 11, pp. 741ff. Often considered the best of Hrotsvit's plays (see, for example, Gundlach, *Deutsche Heldenlieder*, 1970, p. 271), *Abraham* was the first to be translated into German by Adam Werner von Themar in 1503.

parents, for whom I bear great affection, for whom I feel sorry/ and on whose account I tire myself with constant worry./

Effrem: And what are the cares of this world to you, you who have triumphed over the world's vainglory?/

Abraham: This is my worry: that the immense radiance of her beauty should wane/ and be dimmed by some pollution's stain./

Effrem: Such concern will earn no blame./

Abraham: I hope that it'll be so.

Effrem: How old is she?

Abraham: When the course of this year is completed, she will have breathed the breath of life for two Olympiades.[3]

Effrem: An immature girl./

Abraham: That's the reason for my concern./

Effrem: Where does she dwell?/

Abraham: In my own cell./ When asked by her relatives, I undertook to raise her, but decided to bequeath her wealth to the poor.[4]

Effrem: Contempt for worldly things befits the soul intent on heaven.

Abraham: I desire passionately that she be espoused to Christ and that for His service she be trained./

Effrem: An aim worthy to be praised./

Abraham: I am forced to do so by her name.

Effrem: What is she called?

Abraham: Mary.

Effrem: Is that so? The excellence of such an exalted name/ deserves virginity's garland and acclaim./

Abraham: I am convinced that by our kind exhortations and aid,/ she will prove easy to persuade./

Effrem: Let us go to her and let us instill in her mind the desirable security of the virginal life.

---

3 I.e., she is in her eighth year. As Sandro Sticca in "Hrotsvitha's Abraham and Exegetical Tradition" (p. 359) observes, the "not quite eight" is quite important: "One becomes immediately aware of the underlying ontological principle of the not yet eight symbolism. It is a principle directed to personal being and personal activity. If she is not eight yet, Maria, then, is still seven. Patristic and medieval number allegories observed that seven—composed of four, the number of the body, and of three, the number of the soul — expresses the extent of human life and it pertains to human activity; it masks off immediate experience and temporal preoccupation. The fact that Maria is moving toward her eighth year indicates movement in the right direction; she is moving, chronologically, from an imperfect state of temporality to a state of fuller spiritual realization."

4 Abraham's spiritual adoption of Mary brings with itself the cares of a natural father.

*

Abraham:	Oh my adopted daughter, oh part of my soul, Mary, heed my fatherly admonitions/ and my companion Effrem's beneficial instructions./ Strive to imitate in your chasity/ her who is the fount of virginity/ and whose name you bear.
Effrem:	It would be most unfitting that you, daughter, who are joined to Mary,/ the mother of God, through your name's secret mystery/ and have been, thereby,/ raised to the axis of the sky/ among the stars that never set, should wish to debase yourself in your actions and sink to the lowest realms of the world.
Mary:	I am ignorant of the secret of my name;/ therefore, I do not grasp the meaning of what you say/ in such a roundabout way./
Effrem:	Mary means *stella maris*, the "star of the sea," around which, as you may learn,/ the earth is borne and the poles both turn./[5]
Mary:	Why is it called the "star of the sea"?
Effrem:	Because it never sets but is the bright light-source/ that guides sailors on the path of the right course./
Mary:	But how could it ever happen that I, such a little thing and made of clay, could, through my own merits, attain to that glorious place/ where the mysterious symbol of my name resides in grace?/
Effrem:	Through the unimpaired wholeness of your body and the pure holiness of your mind.
Mary:	What great honor for a mortal to equal the rays of stars!
Effrem:	For if you remain uncorrupt and a virgin, you will become the equal of God's angels; surrounded by them, when you have cast off the burden of your body, you will traverse the sky,/ rising above the ether high,/ and journey through the circle of the zodiac, not slowing down or delaying your flight/ until you have reached great delight/ in the arms of

Pandora's origins

---

[5] Hrotsvit's source does not contain this "etymology lesson." The "etymology lesson" introduces the central ideas of the play, those of hope and the workings out of God's plan in Creation and a wide spectrum of images raised by the implications of the name. These recur throughout the play and help to unify the plot by permeating many of the scenes with echoes of the *stella maria* imagery. See Sticca, "Hrotswitha's *Abraham*," pp. 370–74. See also my "Hrotsvit's *Abraham*: The Lesson in Etymology," *Germanic Notes* 16:1 (1985): 2–4.

the virgin's Son, and are embraced by Him in the luminous wedding chamber of His mother./

Mary: Whoever undervalues this is no other/ but a donkey./ Therefore I renounce the world and deny myself so that I may deserve to be bequeathed the joys of such great felicity./

[handwritten marginalia: why donkey?]

Effrem: Behold, the child's heart brings forth the mature wisdom of age./

Abraham: It is by the grace of God that she is so sage./

Effrem: No one can deny this.

Abraham: Yet even though God's grace has been made manifest, it would not be prudent to leave such a young child to her own counsel.

Effrem: That is true.

Abraham: Therefore, I shall build her a little cell, narrow of entrance and adjacent to my own dwelling. I will visit her often and through the window instruct her in the Psalms and other pages of God's law./

Effrem: Rightly so./

Mary: I commit myself, Father Effrem, to your guidance.

Effrem: May the Heavenly Bridegroom, to whose affection you have pledged yourself at such a tender age, succor you, daughter, from all the guiles of Satan.

*

Abraham: Brother Effrem, whenever anything happens to me, either fortune or misery, to you I come, you alone I consult; so do not turn away from the laments I utter/ but help me in the pain I suffer./

Effrem: Abraham, Abraham, what a heart-rending sight./ Why are you more dejected than is meet and right?/ A hermit should never be perturbed/ in the manner of men in the world./

Abraham: My distress is incomparable./ My grief is intolerable!/

Effrem: Don't keep me in suspense with your circumlocutions, but explain what occurred.

Abraham: Mary, my adopted daughter, whom for twice ten years I brought up to the best of my ability, whom I instructed to the best of my skill . . .

Effrem: What happened to her whom you so clearly cherished?/

Abraham: Woe is me, she has perished./

[handwritten marginalia: death of soul = sinning]

Effrem:	How?
Abraham:	In great wretchedness; then she stole away, secretly.
Effrem:	With what tricks did the guile of the ancient serpent beset her?
Abraham:	Through the forbidden passion of a certain deceiver/ who, disguised as a monk, often came to see her/ under the pretense of instructive visits, until with his devilish art/ he ignited the undisciplined instincts of her youthful heart/ to burn in love for him, so much so that she jumped from her window to perform that awful deed.
Effrem:	Ah, I shudder to hear it.
Abraham:	And when the wretched girl, so beguiled,/ found herself lapsed and defiled,/ she beat her breasts,/ lacerated her face and her hands,/ tore her clothes amid sighs,/ pulled out her hair, and raised her voice in lamentations to the skies./
Effrem:	Not without reason, for her ruin must be mourned/ and with great outpouring of tears deplored./
Abraham:	She bewailed not to be what she was.
Effrem:	Poor girl, alas!
Abraham:	She mourned that she had acted against our admonitions.
Effrem:	Rightly so.
Abraham:	Because she had rendered void the toils of her vigils, prayers and fastings, she lamented and raved./
Effrem:	If she had persevered in such great remorse, she would have been saved./
Abraham:	She did not persevere for long/ but added worse to prior wrong./
Effrem:	In fear my stomach is turned;/ my limbs are all unnerved./
Abraham:	For after she had punished herself with these laments, defeated by the immenseness of her grief, she was carried headlong into the lap of desperation./
Effrem:	Alas, alas, what grave perdition!/
Abraham:	And because she despaired of ever attaining forgiveness, she chose to return to the world and to serve its vanity./
Effrem:	Well, up until now, the spirits of iniquity/ had been unaccustomed to gain such victory/ in the abode where hermits stay./
Abraham:	But now we are the demons' prey./
Effrem:	I wonder how it could have happened that, unnoticed by you, she got away./
Abraham:	For some days I was much troubled by the horror of a revelation,/ a vision,/ which, if my mind had not been careless, would have foretold me of her perdition./

madness [handwritten annotation with brace spanning the "And when the wretched girl..." passage]

Effrem:	I would like to know the nature of this vision./
Abraham:	I thought I stood before the entrance of my cell,/ when, behold, there came a dragon of miraculous size and of foul smell/ that rushed with great speed towards a little white dove near me. He snatched up the dove, devoured it and then suddenly vanished.[6]
Effrem:	A vision with clear meaning.
Abraham:	But, I, when I roused myself from the vision, thought about what I had seen and was gripped with terror that a persecution threatened the church which might lead some of the faithful into error./
Effrem:	That would be a cause for terror./
Abraham:	Therefore, prostrate in prayer, I beseeched Him who has foreknowledge of future events to unveil for me the meaning of the sight./
Effrem:	You did right./
Abraham:	Then on the third night,/ when I gave my exhausted body to sleep,/ I thought I saw the very same dragon crushed under my feet,/ wallowing deep,/ and I saw the same white dove, unhurt, dart away./
Effrem:	I am delighted to hear this because without doubt, your daughter Mary will return some day./
Abraham:	When I awoke, I smoothed my prior grief with the solace of this new vision, and collected myself to remember my pupil; then I also recalled, not without sadness, that I had not heard her recite her customary prayers for the last two days.
Effrem:	You remembered too late.
Abraham:	I confess it. Then I approached her cell, knocked on her window and repeatedly called my daughter by name./
Effrem:	Alas, you called in vain./
Abraham:	I did not realize that yet, so I asked her why she was neglecting her prayers, but I received not the slightest sound of response, much to my concern./
Effrem:	What did you do in turn?/
Abraham:	When I understood, at last,/ that she whom I sought had left, I was aghast;/ my innermost parts trembled with fear, and my limbs quaked with terror./

6 Sticca, "Hrotswitha's *Abraham*," pp. 633–38, calls attention to the striking symbolism of the Abraham-Christ analogy throughout the play, especially as it concerns Abraham's two visions, as well as his role as Divine Shepherd.

Effrem:	No wonder!/ Indeed, even now, listening to you I feel the same sensation.
Abraham:	Then I filled the air with doleful sounds asking what wolf had snatched away my lamb, what thief had stolen my child?
Effrem:	You were right to bewail the loss of her whom you have raised.
Abraham:	Then people came who knew for sure/ that what I have now told you is actually true,/ and they said that she had given herself over to sin.
Effrem:	Where is she gone?
Abraham:	It is not known./
Effrem:	What will you do next?/
Abraham:	I have a loyal friend who, without rest,/ is traveling through villages and towns and will not stop until he discovers whereto she is bound./
Effrem:	What if she is found?/
Abraham:	I will change my habit and will go to her disguised as a lover. Perchance, admonished by me,/ she may return after her awful shipwreck to the safe port of earlier tranquillity./
Effrem:	And what will you do/ if meat to eat and wine to drink be placed before you?
Abraham:	I will not refuse them so that I won't be recognized.
Effrem:	Indeed it is praiseworthy that you should use correct discretion in saving the erring girl for Christ, even if it means that you will have to relax the strict rules of our monastic practice.
Abraham:	I am all the more eager to undertake this daring deed now that I know that you are in agreement with me.
Effrem:	He who knows the secrets of our hearts, and knows the intents that underlie our actions, does not disapprove when one of us relaxes temporarily the rigor of our strict rules and behaves like our weaker brethren, if it is done so that he may all the more efficiently regain a soul that has strayed into sin.
Abraham:	Meanwhile, it will be your task to assist me with prayer so that I will not be impeded by the Devil's guiles.
Effrem:	May that greatest of all goods, without which no other good may be, bring your intent to good ends.

*

Abraham:	Is this my friend whom I sent out two years ago to find Mary?/ Yes, it is he!/
Friend:	Greetings, venerable father.
Abraham:	Greetings, dear friend. Long have I waited and I even lost hope of your return.
Friend:	The reason I took so long was that I did not wish to agitate you with unconfirmed news; but as soon as I could investigate and the truth learn,/ I promptly hurried to return./
Abraham:	Did you see Mary?
Friend:	I did.
Abraham:	Where?
Friend:	In a city, close by./
Abraham:	With whom does she reside, on whom does she rely?/
Friend:	It hurts me to reply./
Abraham:	Why?/
Friend:	It is too awful to say./
Abraham:	But tell me, I pray./
Friend:	She has chosen to stay/ with a certain procurer who treats her with tender love. And not without profit, for he receives large sums of money from her lovers every day./
Abraham:	From Mary's lovers?/
Friend:	Yes, from them.
Abraham:	Who are her lovers?/
Friend:	There are many./
Abraham:	Woe is me!/ O, good Jesus, what misfortune is this I hear, that she, whom I raised to be Thy bride/ has strange lovers at her side?/
Friend:	This has been the custom of whores throughout the ages:/ that they delight in the love of strangers./
Abraham:	Bring me a soldier's garb and a good horse so that, after I lay aside my religious habit, I may go to her, disguised as a lover, with all speed./
Friend:	Here is all you need./
Abraham:	Give me a hat also to hide my tonsure.
Friend:	This, too, is very necessary/ so as not to reveal your identity./
Abraham:	Should I take this coin I have to give to the innkeeper?
Friend:	Otherwise you won't be able to meet with Mary.

*

Abraham:	Greetings, good host!/
Innkeeper:	Who calls?/ Greetings!
Abraham:	Do you have a nice place for a traveler to stay overnight?/
Innkeeper:	Indeed we do; our hospitality extends to all who alight./
Abraham:	Good!
Innkeeper:	Come in, so that dinner can be prepared for you./
Abraham:	I owe you much for this merry welcome, but I ask for even more from you./
Innkeeper:	Tell me what you desire, so that I may fulfill it.
Abraham:	Here, take this little gold for the deal;/ and arrange for the most beautiful girl who, as I hear, stays with you, to share our meal./
Innkeeper:	Why do you wish to see her?
Abraham:	I would delight in getting to know her whose beauty I have heard praised by so many and so often.
Innkeeper:	Whoever praised her beauty did not tell a lie, for in the loveliness of her face she outshines all other women.
Abraham:	That is why I yearn for her love.
Innkeeper:	I wonder that in your old age you desire the love of a young woman.
Abraham:	For sure, I come for no other purpose but to see her.

*

Innkeeper:	Come, Mary, come along. Show your beauty to our newcomer.
Mary:	Here I am.
Abraham:	What boldness, what constancy of mind I must muster as I see her whom I raised in my hidden hermitage decked out in a harlot's garb./ But this is not the time to show in my face what is in my heart;/ I must be on guard:/ I will bravely suppress my tears gushing forth, like a man. With feigned cheerfulness of countenance I will veil the bitterness of my internal grief.
Innkeeper:	Lucky Mary, be merry,/ because now not only men your age flock hither, as before, but even men of ripe old age seek your favors. It is you whom they querry./
Mary:	I will not only give you a taste of sweet kisses/ but will caress your ancient neck with close embraces./
Abraham:	That is what I am after.

Mary:	What is it I feel? What is this spell?/ What is this rare and wonderful odor I smell?/ Oh, the smell of this fragrance reminds me of the fragrance of chastity I once practiced!
Abraham:	Now, now I must pretend, now I must persist, now I must be lustful in the manner of lewd young men and play the game/ so that I am not recognized by my seriousness or else she might leave and hide for shame./
Mary:	Woe is me, wretched woman! How I sank, how I fell into perdition's pit!/
Abraham:	This is not a fit place for complaints, where jolly guests sit./
Innkeeper:	Lady Mary, why do you sigh? Why do you cry? In the two years you have lived here, I never heard such grieving, not even a trace./
Mary:	Oh, I wish I could have died three years ago!/ Then I would not have sunk into such disgrace!/
Abraham:	I didn't come all this way/ to join you in lamenting your sins, but to be joined to you making love and being gay./
Mary:	I was moved by a slight regret to utter such words; but let us now dine and be merry/ because, as you admonished me,/ this is certainly not the time to bewail one's sins.
Abraham:	Abundantly we have wined,/ abundantly we have dined,/ and are now tipsy, good host, with generous portions you served. Give us now leave to rise from the table/ so that I might be able/ to lay down and refresh my weary body by sweet rest./
Innkeeper:	I'll do as you request./
Mary:	Rise, my lord, rise up. I shall accompany you to your bedroom.
Abraham:	That pleases me. In fact, I could not have been forced to go, were I not going with you.

*

Mary:	Here is a bedroom for us to stay in. Here is the bed, decked with rich and lovely coverlets. Sit down, so that I may take off your shoes and then you won't have to tire yourself removing them.
Abraham:	First, lock the door so that no one may enter.
Mary:	Don't worry on that account. I will make sure/ that the bolt is secure,/ and that no one finds easy access to disturb us.
Abraham:	Now the time has come to remove my hat and reveal who

	I am. Oh my adoptive daughter, oh part of my soul, Mary,/ don't you recognize me,/ the old man who raised you like a father and who pledged you with a ring/ to the only begotten Son of the Heavenly King?/
Mary:	Woe is me! It is my father and teacher Abraham who speaks!
Abraham:	What happened to you, my daughter Mary?/
Mary:	Tremendous misery./
Abraham:	Who deceived you!/ Who seduced you?/
Mary:	He who overthrew our first parents too./
Abraham:	Where is that angelic life that already here on earth you led?/
Mary:	Destroyed, it fled./
Abraham:	Where is the modesty of your virginity? Where your admirable countenance?/
Mary:	Lost and gone from hence./
Abraham:	What reward for the efforts of your fasting, prayers, and vigils can you hope for unless you return to your senses, you who fell/ from the height of Heaven and have sunk into the depths of Hell?/
Mary:	Woe is me, alas!
Abraham:	Why did you disdain me?/ Why did you desert me?/ Why did you not tell me of your wretched sin, so that I and my beloved friend Effrem could perform worthy penance for you?
Mary:	After I first sinned, and sank into perfidy,/ I did not dare, polluted as I was, to even approach your sanctity./
Abraham:	Who ever has lived free from sin except for the Virgin's Son?/
Mary:	No one./
Abraham:	It is human to err but evil to persist in sin; he who fell suddenly is not the one to be blamed,/ only he who fails to rise promptly again./
Mary:	Woe is me, wretched woman.
Abraham:	Why do you fall down?/ Why do you stay immobile lying on the ground?/ Arise and hear what I have to say!/
Mary:	I fell, shaken with fear, because I could not bear the force of your fatherly admonitions' sway./
Abraham:	Consider my love for you and put aside your fears./
Mary:	I cannot; I cannot cease my tears./
Abraham:	Did I not relinquish my accustomed hermitage on your behalf, and did I not leave aside all observance of our regular rule,/ so much so, that I who am an old hermit,

	have turned into a pleasure-seeking lewd fool,/ and I, who for so long practiced silence, made jokes and spoke merry words so that I wouldn't be recognized? Why do you still stare at the ground with lowered face? Why do you refuse to speak with me?
Mary:	I am troubled by my grave offense;/ this is why I don't dare to presume to lift my eyes to Heaven or have the confidence/ to speak with you.
Abraham:	Don't lose faith, my daughter, but abandon the abyss of dejection and place your hope in God.
Mary:	The enormity of my sins has cast me into the depths of despair.
Abraham:	Your sins are grave, I admit,/ but heavenly pity is greater than any sin we may commit./ Therefore cast off your despair and beware of leaving unused this short time given to you for penitence. Know that Divine Grace abounds even where the abomination of sins prevails.
Mary:	If I had any hope of receiving forgiveness, my eagerness to do penance would burst forth.
Abraham:	Have mercy on my exhaustion, which I incurred on your account, cast off this dangerous and sinful despair, which we know to be a graver offense than all other sins. For whoever despairs, thinking that God would not come to the aid of sinners, that person sins irremediably. Because just as the spark from a flintstone cannot set the sea on fire,/ so the bitter taste of our sins cannot likewise aspire/ to alter the sweetness of Divine goodwill.
Mary:	It is not the magnificence of Heavenly Grace which I doubt, but when I consider the enormity of my own sin, then I fear that the performance of even a worthy penance will not suffice.
Abraham:	I take your sins upon myself; only come back to the place which you deserted/ and take up again the life which you subverted./
Mary:	I will never go against any of your wishes but will embrace obediently all your commandments.
Abraham:	Now, I believe that you are my child, whom I raised; now I feel that you are the one to be loved above all others.
Mary:	I possess some clothes and a little gold;/ I wait to be told/ how to dispose of them.
Abraham:	What you acquired through sin/ must be cast off together with the sins./

Mary:	I thought, perhaps, they could be offered to the sacred altar or be given to the poor./
Abraham:	It is neither sanctioned nor acceptable that gifts be given to God which were acquired through sin and are impure./
Mary:	Beyond this, I have no concern./
Abraham:	Dawn arrives; the day breaks. Let us return!/
Mary:	You, beloved father, must lead the way/ as the good shepherd leads the sheep gone astray;/ and I, advancing in your footsteps, will follow your lead./
Abraham:	Not so; I will proceed on foot but you will ride on my horse so that the sharp rocks of the road will not hurt your tender little feet./
Mary:	What shall I say? How shall I ever repay your kindness? You do not force me, miserable wretch, with threats, but exhort me to do penance with kindness.
Abraham:	I ask nothing of you, except that you remain intent upon spending the rest of your life in God's service.
Mary:	Out of my own free will I shall remain contrite,/ I shall persist in my penance with all my might,/ and even if I lose the ability to perform the act,/ the will to do it shall never lack./
Abraham:	It is important that you serve the Divine will as eagerly as you served worldly vanities./
Mary:	The will of the Lord be done in me, because of your merits./
Abraham:	Let us return and hurry on our way./
Mary:	Let us hurry, I am weary of delay./

*

Mary:	With what speed we have traveled over this difficult and rugged road!/
Abraham:	Whatever is done with devotion is accomplished with ease. Behold, here is your deserted abode./
Mary:	Woe is me, this cell is witness to my sin; therefore I fear to enter./
Abraham:	That's understandable. Any place where the ancient enemy has won a triumph is to be avoided forever./
Mary:	And where do you intend me to stay and perform my penance?
Abraham:	Go into the small interior room so that the ancient serpent will not find another opportunity to deceive you.

Mary:	I will not contradict you but embrace eagerly what you command.
Abraham:	I shall go to Effrem, my friend, so that he, who alone mourned with me over your loss, may rejoice with me over your return./
Mary:	A worthy concern!/

*

Effrem:	Are you bringing me joyous news?/
Abraham:	Most joyous news./
Effrem:	I am glad. Doubtlessly you have found Mary.
Abraham:	Indeed I found her and led her back, rejoicing, to the fold./
Effrem:	I believe this was done by the grace of God./
Abraham:	I doubt it not.
Effrem:	I would like to know how she will conduct her life from this day on and how she will fulfill her penance?/
Abraham:	Entirely according to my governance./
Effrem:	That will be of great advantage to her.
Abraham:	Whatever I have suggested, however difficult, however harsh, she has not refused to do it.
Effrem:	Very praiseworthy.
Abraham:	She wears a hair-shirt and is weakened by the constant exercise of vigils and fastings, but still she forces her tender body to follow her soul's mandate/ and observes the strictest rules, bearing penance's weight./
Effrem:	It is only right/ that the filth of her sinful delight/ be purged by the bitter severity of her plight./
Abraham:	Whoever hears her lamentation is wounded in his heart by its force;/ whoever feels the pangs of her remorse/ himself feels remorse./
Effrem:	It usually happens so.
Abraham:	She works with all her strength to become an example of conversion/ to those for whom she was the cause of perdition./
Effrem:	That is proper contrition./
Abraham:	She strives to appear as brightly radiant as she was once foul.
Effrem:	I rejoice in hearing this.
Abraham:	And justifiably so, for even the angelic choirs rejoice and praise the Lord when sinners repent.
Effrem:	No wonder, for the steadfast perseverance of the just man delights Him no more than the penance of a sinner.

Abraham: He should be all the more praised for this gain,/ as there was little hope for her return to her former self again./

Effrem: Rejoicing let us praise, and by praising let us glorify the only begotten Son of God, honored and exalted, who does not wish that those whom He redeemed with His precious blood should ever perish.

Abraham: His be all honor and glory, praise and jubilation, for time everlasting, Amen.

Martyrdom of the Holy Virgins
Fides, Spes, and Karitas

(Sapientia)[1]

The martyrdom of the holy virgins Fides, Spes and Karitas who are killed
by the Emperor Diocletian after great torture in the presence of Sapientia,
their venerable mother, who exhorts them maternally/ to bear their
martyrdom bravely. This saintly mother, Sapientia, after her daughters'
sacrifices,/ recovers their bodies and embalms them with diverse spices./
She buries them with honor at the third milestone outside of Rome/ and,
having spent forty days in holy prayers at their graves, her soul departs
for its heavenly home./

*

Antiochus: In the hope that Your Highness, Emperor Hadrian, achieve
prosperity and success according to your wishes and that
your state may flourish in happiness and without disturbance, I have always desired to uproot immediately/ and
destroy entirely/ whatever might harm the state, whatever
might threaten its peace and tranquility./

Hadrian: Rightly so, as our prosperity is the cause for your good
fortune since we increase your rank and standing daily./

Antiochus: I am grateful to Your Highness. Therefore, whenever I
discover anything that appears subversive or brings conten-
tion,/ I do not hide it but bring it immediately to your
attention./

Hadrian: And justly so, so that you avoid doing what is forbidden/
by hiding what should not be hidden./

Antiochus: I have never been guilty of committing such a crime./

Hadrian: I know that. But tell me if you have discovered anything
new this time./

---

[1] Cf. *Acta Sancrtorum*, August 1, pp. 16ff. The girls personify the gifts of the Holy Ghost often
discussed in patristic literature (cf. Saint Augustine, *De Fide, Spe et Caritate*, Patrologia
Latina 40).

Antiochus:	Recently a certain woman arrived in Rome,/ not alone/ but accompanied by her three little children./
Hadrian:	Of what sex are the children?/
Antiochus:	They are all girls.
Hadrian:	Could the arrival of these three little girls possibly present a danger for the state?/
Antiochus:	The danger is great./
Hadrian:	Why?/
Antiochus:	Peace is disturbed thereby./
Hadrian:	How can that be?
Antiochus:	What could possibly disrupt the harmony of civic peace more than religious dissent?
Hadrian:	Nothing is graver, nothing more dangerous. The Roman Empire testifies to that fact,/ infected everywhere by the mortal plague of the Christian sect./
Antiochus:	This woman whom I just mentioned exhorts our citizens and clients/ to abandon the ancestral and ancient rites/ and to convert to Christianity.
Hadrian:	Do her exhortations succeed?/
Antiochus:	They do so, indeed!/ Our wives despise us so that they refuse to eat with us,/ or even more to sleep with us./
Hadrian:	I admit that poses a danger./
Antiochus:	Your Highness should take some preventative measures as concerns this stranger./
Hadrian:	You are right./ Have her arraigned and questioned in our sight/ to see whether she might change her mind./
Antiochus:	Do you wish me to bring her to you?/
Hadrian:	Certainly I do./

*

Antiochus:	Foreign woman, what's your name?
Sapientia:	Sapientia.
Antiochus:	Emperor Hadrian orders you to come to court and appear before him.
Sapientia:	I do not fear to enter the palace in the noble company of my daughters, nor do I fear looking upon the Emperor's threatening face./
Antiochus:	This hateful Christian race/ is always bent on spurning our ruler's authority.
Sapientia:	The Ruler of the Universe, who never can be conquered, will not permit the fiend to overcome His people.

Antiochus: Bridle your tongue/ and hurry now along./

Sapientia: Go ahead, and show the way;/ we shall follow without delay./

*

Antiochus: Behold the Emperor seated on his throne; be careful of what you say.

Sapientia: Christ's command preempts that need/ for He promised us gifts of wisdom, always to succeed./

Hadrian: Come hither, Antiochus.

Antiochus: Here I am, my lord.

Hadrian: Are these the little women whom you denounced as Christians?

Antiochus: Yes.

Hadrian: The beauty of every one of them stuns my senses;/ I cannot stop admiring the nobility of their bearing, their many excellences./[2]

Antiochus: Desist from admiring them, my lord, and force them to worship our gods.

Hadrian: What if I mollify them first with flattering speech?/ Perhaps they will then give in, one and each./

Antiochus: That would be much better, for the female sex's fragility/ makes it prone to yield to flattery./

Hadrian: Noble lady, I invite you amiably and kindly to worship our gods and so enjoy our friendship./

Sapientia: I don't care to satisfy your wish by worshiping your gods, nor do I seek your friendship./

Hadrian: Having controlled my anger, I am not indignant but am concerned with fatherly care/ for you and your daughters' welfare./

Sapientia: My children, do not open your hearts to the tricks of this devilish snake;/ scorn him as I do for Christ's sake./

Fides: We despise him in our souls and scorn the nonsense he utters.

Hadrian: What are you whispering? What are you saying that is not to be heard?/

Sapientia: I spoke to my daughters and only a word./

---

2 Almost inevitably the virtue and chastity of Hrotsvit's heroines are reflected in their external beauty and nobility of bearing.

Hadrian:	You appear to be of noble descent. I would like to know from where you came,/ who are your ancestors, and what is your name?/
Sapientia:	Even though pride in our noble descent is of little consequence to us, I do not deny to trace/ my birth from an illustrious race./
Hadrian:	I can believe that that be the case./
Sapientia:	My ancestors were eminent princes of Italy and Sapientia is my name./
Hadrian:	The splendor of your noble ancestry illumines your face;/ and wisdom, inherent in your name, flows in your speech's grace./
Sapientia:	You flatter us in vain;/ your attempt to sway us will reap no gain./
Hadrian:	Tell me why you came here, and why you incite our people, subverting our reign?/
Sapientia:	For no other matter/ but to be a witness to truth, to understand the faith, which you persecute, better,/ and to consecrate my daughters to Christ.
Hadrian:	Tell me their names.
Sapientia:	One is called Fides, the second Spes, the third Karitas.
Hadrian:	How old are they?/
Sapientia:	Would it please you, children, if I fatigued this fool/ with a lesson in arithmetical rule?/[3]
Fides:	Yes, mother, it would it please us greatly,/ and we too would hear it gladly./
Sapientia:	O, Emperor, you wish to know my children's ages; Karitas has completed a diminished, evenly even number of years;/ Spes, on the other hand, a diminished evenly uneven number; and Karitas an augmented unevenly even number of years./
Hadrian:	Your reply leaves me totally ignorant as to the answer to my question./
Sapientia:	That is no wonder since not only a single number but several fall into the categories I mentioned./

---

[3] Hadrian, who is called a fool, is apparently ignorant of arithmetical properties. Yet this Emperor is particularly reputed to have been well educated, especially in mathematics (cf. Homeyer, *Opera*, p. 353). As Sticca observes, "Comic Realism," p. 131, reflecting on the passage, "At times, the comic element in her plays takes the form of syllogistic argumentation destined to underline the disparity that exists between the ludicrous ignorance of the persecutors and the subtle and refined knowledge of the Christian martyrs."

Hadrian: Explain it in more detail/ or my mind will try to grasp it to no avail./

Sapientia: Karitas has completed two Olympiades,/ Spes two lustra, and Fides, three Olympiades./

Hadrian: And why are the number eight, which constitutes two Olympiades, and the number ten, which denotes two lustra, called diminished numbers?/ And why is the number twelve, which covers three Olympiades, designated as an augmented number?/[4]

Sapientia: All numbers are called diminished whose parts, when added up, amount to a sum less than the number itself of which they constitute a part. Thus, for example, the number eight has as its half four, its fourth two, and its eighth one./ These, added up make seven as a sum./ Similarly, the number ten has as its half five, its fifth two, and its tenth one, which when added, amount to eight. Augmented numbers, on the other hand, are those whose parts are greater than the number itself, as, for example, twelve, for half of twelve is six, a third is four, a fourth is three, a sixth is two and a twelfth is one, all of which add up to sixteen. But I should not leave unmentioned the principal numbers – that is, those that hold the middle position between these unequal, incommensurate numbers,/ and those which are called "perfect numbers."/ These have parts that are neither larger nor smaller than the number itself,/ such as the number six, whose parts, three, two, and one, add up to exactly the same sum as the number itself./ For the same reason twenty-eight, four hundred ninety-six, and eight thousand one hundred twenty-eight are called perfect numbers./

Hadrian: And how about the rest of the numbers?

Sapientia: They are all either augmented or diminished.

Hadrian: And what is meant by an evenly even number?

Sapientia: Evenly even is a number which can be divided into two equal parts/ and whose parts, in turn, can be divided into two equal parts,/ until one reaches an indivisible number. Such numbers are eight and sixteen, too,/ as well as all of their multiples by two./

Hadrian: And what is an evenly uneven number?

---

4 The mathematics lesson is based on excerpts from Boethius's *De Institutio Arithmetica*, I.

Sapientia: Evenly uneven numbers are those that can be divided into equal parts but whose parts are indivisible, prime numbers./ Such a number is ten, as are all those formed by doubling prime numbers./ Evenly uneven numbers are the exact opposite of the evenly even numbers,/ because in the first the smaller term can be divided, but in the other only the larger term is divisible; also, in the first all parts of the number are evenly even – both the denominator and the quotient – but in the other, if the denominator is even, the quotient is uneven;/ if the quotient is even, the denominator is uneven./

Hadrian: I don't know what is meant by term, denominator or quotient.

Sapientia: When several numbers are arranged in order, then the first is called a lesser term, and the last a greater term: when, however, we divide by a number, we call that number the denominator or divisor; when we count the number of the divided part, we call it the quotient.

Hadrian: And what is an unevenly even number?

Sapientia: Unevenly even numbers are those that, like the evenly even numbers, can be divided not only once but twice, and frequently even three times or more, without arriving at an indivisible unit.

Hadrian: What a thorough, perplexing lecture has arisen from my simple question concerning the children's ages!

Sapientia: Praise be thereof to the supreme wisdom of the Creator/ and to the marvelous science of this world's Maker,/ who not only created the world in the beginning out of nothing and ordered everything according to number, measure and weight,/ but also in the seasons and in the ages of men gave us the ability to grasp the wondrous science of the arts.[5]

Hadrian: For long I bore your discourse so as to make you ready to comply now./

Sapientia: How?/

Hadrian: By worshiping the gods.

Sapientia: That I will never consent to do.

Hadrian: If you refuse, you will have to be forced with tortures.

---

[5]   Wisdom 11:21.

Sapientia:	You may lacerate my body with the weapons you wield,/ but you will never succeed in compelling my soul to yield./
Antiochus:	The day is ending, night is near./ This is no time to quarrel; dinner time is here./
Hadrian:	Let them be placed under guard and in prison./ I'll grant them three days to reconsider their position./
Antiochus:	Guard these women closely, soldiers! Don't give them an occasion to escape.
Sapientia:	My sweet little daughters, my darling children, hark!/ Do not be saddened by our prison's dismal dark,/ do not be afraid of the punishments at hand./
Fides:	Our bodies may tremble at the thought of tortures, yet our souls exult in the reward so grand./
Sapientia:	Overcome the softness of your tender years by the strength of mature reflection!/
Spes:	You must support us with your prayers so that we may win perfection./
Sapientia:	That is what I pray for incessantly,/ that is what I ask for and request earnestly:/ that you persevere in your faith, which, from your early childhood on, I tried to instill in your mind without any rest./
Karitas:	We will never forget what we learned in our cradle suckling at your breast./
Sapientia:	It was for this that I nursed you with my milk flowing free;/ it was for this that I carefully reared you three;/ that I may espouse you to a heavenly, not an earthly bridegroom and may deserve to be called the mother-in-law of the Eternal King thereby./
Fides:	For the love of that Bridegroom we are prepared to die./
Sapientia:	Your decision delights me more that the sweet taste of nectar, my dears./
Spes:	Lead us to the judges and you shall promptly see how our love for Him overcomes our fears./
Sapientia:	My only wish is this: that by your virginity I may be crowned/ and by your martyrdom, renowned./
Spes:	Hand in hand, let us go and confound the grim tyrant.
Sapientia:	Wait until the appointed date./
Fides:	Though weary of delay, we shall wait./

*

Hadrian:	Antiochus, have those Italian captives brought before us.
Antiochus:	Come forth Sapientia; you and your children are to appear before the Emperor.
Sapientia:	Come with me, my daughters; be firm,/ persevere in faith that you may blessedly earn/ the palm of martyrdom.
Spes:	We come with all speed and He, for whose love we are led to our death, will accompany us.
Hadrian:	The serenity of Our Majesty granted you three days to reflect upon what's good for you; so yield to our orders and comply!/
Antiochus:	Why do you deign to exchange words with this impertinent woman who keeps insulting you with insolent glee?/
Hadrian:	Should I leave her unpunished, to go free?/
Antiochus:	Of course not.
Hadrian:	Then what should be done?
Antiochus:	Urge those little girls to yield, and if they resist, do not spare their youth, but let them be killed so that their rebellious mother may be tormented all the more acutely by their pain./
Hadrian:	What you suggest I shall ordain./
Antiochus:	So in the end, you shall prevail./
Hadrian:	Fides, look with respect upon the venerable image of great Diana and bring offerings to the holy goddess so that you may possess her favor.
Fides:	O, what a foolish Imperial command; worthy of nothing but contempt!
Hadrian:	What are you mumbling in derision;/ whom are you mocking with your wry expression?/
Fides:	It's your foolishness I deride, and I mock your stupidity./
Hadrian:	My stupidity?/
Fides:	Yes.
Antiochus:	The Emperor's?
Fides:	Yes, his!
Antiochus:	This is abominable!
Fides:	For what is more foolish, what can seem more stupid than your command to show contempt for the Creator of all and venerate base metal instead?/
Antiochus:	Fides, you are mad!/
Fides:	Antiochus, you lie!
Antiochus:	Isn't it the sign of great insanity and of severe madness when you call the ruler of the world a fool?/

Fides:	I have called him a fool,/ I now call him a fool/ and I shall call him a fool/ as long as I live.
Antiochus:	You will not live long; soon you shall expire./
Fides:	To die in Christ is just what I desire./
Hadrian:	Twelve centurions shall flog her limbs – one and each./
Antiochus:	Those are just desserts for her brazen speech./
Hadrian:	O brave centurions, come to the fore/ and avenge the insults that I bore./
Antiochus:	A just punishment./
Hadrian:	Antiochus, ask again if she is willing to repent./
Antiochus:	Will you, Fides, continue to insult the Emperor as before?
Fides:	Why should I be less inclined to do it?/
Antiochus:	Because lashes will make you rue it./
Fides:	Flogging will not make me silent because I will not feel the pain./
Antiochus:	What wretched obstinacy; what insolent audacity again!/
Hadrian:	Her body is ripped open by the flogging but her mind is still puffed up with pride's ambition./
Fides:	You are mistaken, Hadrian, if you think that you are wearying me with these tortures; it is not I but my torturers who are tired, and it is they who reek with sweat from exhaustion./
Hadrian:	Have her nipples cut off, Antiochus, so that through shame at last she may be coerced to relent.
Antiochus:	O, would that she could be somehow coerced!/
Hadrian:	Perhaps she can be forced . . ./
Fides:	You have wounded my chaste breasts, but you have not hurt me. Look, instead of blood, milk gushes forth.
Hadrian:	Have her thrown on a fiery hot grill/ so that the glowing coals will make her still./
Antiochus:	She deserves to die miserably, she who did not fear to scorn you.
Fides:	Whatever you plan for my pain/ becomes the calm of joyful gain;/ so I rest comfortably on the grill,/ as if I were on a peaceful ship./
Hadrian:	Prepare a pot full of wax and pitch; place it on the pyre/ and cast this rebel into the boiling mire!/
Fides:	I'll jump into it out of my free volition./
Hadrian:	Go ahead, with my permission!/
Fides:	Where are your threats now? Look! Unhurt I frolic and swim in the boiling stew,/ and I feel the cool of the early morning dew./

Hadrian:	Antiochus, what is to be done?/
Antiochus:	Make sure that she doesn't escape and run./
Hadrian:	Put her to the sword!/ 5
Antiochus:	Otherwise she will not be defeated.
Fides:	I must now rejoice in the Lord./
Sapientia:	Christ, unconquered victor over Satan, grant my daughter Fides endurance.
Fides:	O, venerable mother, say your last farewell to your child; give a kiss to your firstborn; expel sadness from your heart because I am on my way to eternal rewards.
Sapientia:	O my child, my child, I am not disturbed. I feel no sadness, but I say farewell exulting in you and I kiss your mouth and eyes with tears of joy praying that you preserve the holy mystery of your name, even as you fall under the executioner's blow.
Fides:	O my sisters, born of the same mother, give me a kiss of peace, and prepare yourselves to bear the impending strife./
Spes:	Help us with your constant prayers so that we may deserve to follow you to everlasting life./
Fides:	Obey the admonitions of our saintly parent who has always exhorted us to despise this present world so that we may deserve to attain the Eternal Kingdom.
Karitas:	Gladly we obey our mother's admonitions so that we may reap eternal bliss./
Fides:	Come then, executioner, kill me! Perform your office; don't be remiss./
Sapientia:	I embrace the severed head of my dead daughter, and keep kissing her lips; I thank Thee, Christ, for granting victory/ to a little girl still in infancy./
Hadrian:	Spes, give in to my admonition./ I counsel you in paternal affection./
Spes:	What do you urge me?/ What do you counsel me?/
Hadrian:	That you don't imitate your sister's obstinacy and thus avoid suffering similar pain./
Spes:	O, how I wish to be worthy of her, and imitate her in her pain/ so that, like her, I may achieve similar gain./
Hadrian:	Lay aside this callousness of heart and relent; bring incense to the great Diana. Then I will adopt you as my own child/ and cherish you with all my heart./
Spes:	I don't want you for my father; I have no desire for your favors; therefore, you chase after empty dreams if you think that I shall ever yield to you.

Hadrian:	Watch your speech or you'll feel my ire!/
Spes:	I do not care. Be irate Sire!/
Antiochus:	I wonder, my lord, why you let yourself be scorned by this worthless little girl. I myself am bursting with rage as I hear her bark at you so fearlessly.[6]
Hadrian:	For long I spared her youth but I will not spare her any longer; I'll give her the punishment she deserves.
Antiochus:	O, I wish you would.
Hadrian:	Lictors, come forth! Take this rebel in your grip/ and beat her to death with your heaviest whip./
Antiochus:	Now she will feel the severity of your anger because she cared so little for your kind mildness.
Spes:	But *this* is the kindness I desire; *this* is the mildness I hope for.[7]
Antiochus:	Sapientia, what are you mumbling, standing there with your eyes upturned next to your dead child's body?
Sapientia:	I pray to our eternal Father, that He may grant Spes the same perseverance and strength as he granted Fides.
Spes:	O mother, mother, how efficacious, how useful are the prayers you say!/ Behold, even while you pray,/ my torturers are breathless; they flog me again and again,/ yet I feel not the slightest pain./
Hadrian:	If the lashes don't hurt you,/ harsher punishments will force you./
Spes:	Bring on, bring on whatever cruel, whatever deadly thing you have invented;/ the more savage your punishment, the more you will be confounded when you are defeated./
Hadrian:	She is to be suspended in mid-air and torn to pieces with claws so that when her bowels have been severed/ and her bones have been bared,/ cracking, limb by limb, she dies./[8]
Antiochus:	That is the Emperor's order, and his just reprisal./
Spes:	You speak with the deceit of a fox, Antiochus, and with the werewolf's two-faced cunning.
Antiochus:	Hold your tongue, you wretch; your chatter must end./
Spes:	It will not turn out as you hope, but you and your lord humiliated will stand./

---

6   The animal imagery is deliberate; *latrare* (to bark) is intended as a grave insult to Spes.
7   Hrotsvit is fond of ironic repetition often coupled with anaphora.
8   The tortures devised for the three girls are clearly the most savage of all punishments in the whole drama series. It is a direct reflection of the pagan's frustration at being unable to conquer the spirit of Christians.

Hadrian:	What new fragrance do I smell?/ What amazing sweetness do I sense?/
Spes:	The pieces of my lacerated flesh give off this fragrant heavenly scent,/ forcing you to admit against your will that I cannot be harmed by your punishment./
Hadrian:	Antiochus, what am I to do?/
Antiochus:	Think of tortures anew./
Hadrian:	Place a bronze pot full of oil, wax, fat, and pitch over the flames, and tie her up and throw her in.
Antiochus:	Perhaps when she is given over to Vulcan's force, there'll be no way to escape the fire./
Spes:	Christ's mighty power has been known to change the nature of fire,/ to make its rage harmlessly expire./
Hadrian:	What is it I hear, Antiochus? It sounds like a crashing flood./
Antiochus:	Alas, alas, my lord!/
Hadrian:	What is happening to us? I am alarmed./
Antiochus:	That bubbling hot brew burst the pot, destroyed the servants, and that witch appears to be unharmed./[9]
Hadrian:	I admit defeat./
Antiochus:	Full and complete./
Hadrian:	Behead her!/
Antiochus:	There is no other way to kill her./
Spes:	O beloved Karitas, O, my only sister! Do not fear the tyrant's threat,/ and do not dread his punishments./ Follow in firm faith the example of your sisters, who precede you to Heaven's palace.
Karitas:	I am weary of this life. I am weary of this earthly abode because, though only for a very short time, I'll be separated from you.
Spes:	Lay aside this loathing and concentrate on the prize, for even though we shall be separated for a short time, we shall soon be reunited in Heaven.
Karitas:	Let it be done! Let it be so!
Spes:	Rejoice, good mother, be glad,/ and do not feel sad/ in maternal concern; have hope instead of grief as you see me die for Christ.
Sapientia:	Now I am happy, but later I will exalt in perfect joy when I have sent your little sister to Heaven, martyred like you,/ and when I myself follow you there too./

---

9   Again, the word is *malefica*. Cf. *Dulcitius* XIV, 2.

Spes:	The eternal Holy Trinity will restore to you in everlasting life all three of your daughters.
Sapientia:	Take comfort, my child. Don't be afraid./ The henchman approaches with his naked blade./
Spes:	I welcome the sword. Thou, Christ, accept my soul, separated from its bodily frame,/ for bearing witness to Thy holy name./
Sapientia:	O Karitas, my hope, my darling child, single one left of my womb, do not disappoint your mother, who expects you to win this test of strife./ Spurn the comfort of this life/ so that you may reach never-ending joy, where your sisters already sparkle, radiant with the crowns of untouched virginity.
Karitas:	Stand by me, mother, with your saintly prayers, so that I may be worthy to partake of that bliss./
Sapientia:	I beg you to stay firm in your faith to the very end, and I have no doubt you will be rewarded with heavenly bliss./
Hadrian:	Karitas, I have had more than enough! I am fed up with your sisters' insults and I am rather exasperated with their drawn-out arguments; I will therefore not contend with you for long, but reward you richly with goods if you obey, and punish you if you disobey.
Karitas:	I embrace good with all my heart, and I detest all evil that may be./
Hadrian:	That's a wholesome attitude for you to take and is acceptable to me./ Therefore, by the grace of my kindness, I will require very little of you./
Karitas:	What is it you wish me to do?/
Hadrian:	Simply say "Great Diana" and, beyond that, I will not compel you to procure any sacrifice.
Karitas:	I will certainly not say that.
Hadrian:	Why?
Karitas:	Because I don't wish to lie./ I am born of the same parents as my sisters, imbued by the same sacraments, strengthened by the same firmness of faith. Know, therefore, that we are one and the same in what we want, what we feel and what we think. In nothing will I differ from them.
Hadrian:	How insulting to be held in contempt by a mere child!
Karitas:	I may be young in years, yet I am expert enough to confound you in argument.
Hadrian:	Take her, Antiochus, and have her hung and lashed on a rack. /
Antiochus:	I fear lashes won't be of any use.
Hadrian:	If they are of no use, then order a furnace to be heated for

three continuous days and nights and throw her into the raging fire./ 2

Karitas: What an impotent judge, who cannot overcome an eight-year old infant without the force of fire!/

Hadrian: Go, Antiochus, and carry out my desire!/

Karitas: Even though he will try to comply with your savage decree,/ he will not lacerate my flesh and the flames will neither harm my garments nor my hair./

Hadrian: That is to be seen./

Karitas: I hope that it *will* be seen./

Hadrian: Antiochus, what's the matter? Why do you return, looking dejected?/

Antiochus: As soon as you learn the cause of my gloom, you will be no less affected./

Hadrian: Speak up, don't hide it.

Antiochus: That petulant little girl whom you gave over to me to be tortured was flogged in my presence, but the lashes didn't even scratch her tender skin. Finally, I threw her into the furnace, glowing red-hot with its heat . . ./

Hadrian: Why do you cease to speak?/ Report the outcome.

Antiochus: The flame exploded and burned five thousand men./

Hadrian: And what happened to her then?/

Antiochus: To Karitas?/

Hadrian: Yes.

Antiochus: Playfully she walked among the flame-spewing vapors, quite unhurt,/ and sang hymns of praise to her God. And those who watched her and were alert/ said that three men dressed in white were walking along with her.

Hadrian: I blush to see her again;/ my efforts to harm her are all in vain./

Antiochus: Have her beheaded./ 3

Hadrian: Have it done without delay.

*

Antiochus: Uncover your stubborn neck, Karitas, and prepare for the executioner's sword./

Karitas: In this I do not resist your wish but gladly obey your word./

Sapientia: Now, my child, I must exult, now I must rejoice in Christ's glory;/ no more care and no more worry,/ for I am sure of your victory./

Karitas: Give me a kiss, Mother, and commend my departing soul which He breathed into you from Heaven!

Karitas:	Glory be to Thee, O Christ. Thou hast called me to Thee, elevated by the martyr's palm.
Sapientia:	Farewell, my dearest daughter, and when you are united with Christ in Heaven, remember your mother, having been made patron of her who bore you.[10]

*

Sapientia:	Come, noble ladies, come and help me bury my daughters' remains.
Matrons:	We shall preserve the bodies with spices and celebrate the service with all honors. *floral*
Sapientia:	Great is your kindness and wondrous your support which you show my dead children and me.
Matrons:	Whatever you wish, we shall fulfill with devoted hearts.
Sapientia:	I don't doubt it.
Matrons:	Where is the place that you chose as the burial site?/
Sapientia:	At the third milestone outside of town, if the long distance is all right./[11]
Matrons:	We don't mind a long journey's strain;/ gladly we follow the funeral train./
Sapientia:	Here is the place.
Matrons:	It is worthy to harbor the children's remains.
Sapientia:	I commit to you, Earth, the flowers of my womb. Guard them in your earthen lap until in glory they bloom afresh/ after the resurrection of the flesh./ And thou, Christ, imbue their souls in the meantime with splendorous bliss,/ and grant that their bones may rest in peace./
Matrons:	Amen.
Sapientia:	I am grateful for your kindness in my great loss and for the consolation you convey./
Matrons:	Do you wish for us to stay?/
Sapientia:	No.
Matrons:	Why not?
Sapientia:	I don't wish for you to incur any more trouble on my behalf. Go forth in peace, and return safely – it is enough that you stayed with me three nights long./

---

10 The patronship function of saints, especially martyrs, is often emphasized in Hrotsvit's works. Cf. *Pelagius, Basilius, Gongolf.* The girls, having suffered martyrdom, rise above their mother in spiritual worth and can intercede for her.

11 The distance is not known exactly; it is between eighteen and twenty-two miles. See Homeyer, *Opera*, p. 373.

Matrons:	Are you not coming along?/
Sapientia:	No.
Matrons:	What do you plan to do?/
Sapientia:	To remain here. Perhaps what I desire will be fulfilled. Perhaps my wish will come true./
Matrons:	What do you pray for; what do you desire?/
Sapientia:	Only that when my prayers are completed, in Christ I may expire./
Matrons:	We will stay until we have buried you; then we will retire./
Sapientia:	As you wish. Adonai Emmanuel, whom before all times God, the Father of all, created and whom in our own time the Virgin Mother bore; one Christ, of two natures but the duality of natures not dividing the unity of the one person, and the unity of the person not lessening the diversity of Thy two natures. Let the lovely angels' choir their voices raise/ and may the sweet harmony of the stars exult Thee in jubilant praise;/ let all that is knowable through science praise Thee,/ and all that is made of the material of the four elements exult Thee,/ because Thou alone with the Father and the Holy Ghost/ are made form without matter, begotten by the Father with the Holy Ghost./ Thou didst not scorn to become man, capable of human suffering,/ while Thy divinity remained oblivious to suffering,/ so that all who believe in Thee should not perish in eternal strife,/ but have the joy of everlasting life;/ Thou hast not refused to taste death for us, only to destroy it by rising again from the dead./ Very God and very man,/ I know that Thou hast said that Thou wilt reward a hundredfold/ all of those who gave up the hold/ of worldly possessions and earthly love for the worship of Thy name,/ and Thou hast promised to the same/ to bestow upon them the gift of life everlasting. Inspired by the hope of this promise, I followed Thy command, freely offering up the children I bore./ Therefore do not Thou delay any more/ to keep Thy promise, and free me quickly from the fetters of my earthly body, so that I may rejoice in the heavenly reception of my daughters, whose sacrifice I didn't prolong,/ and exult in their new joyful lauding song/ as they follow the Paschal Lamb in the midst of other maidens./ And even though I cannot join them in chanting the canticles of virginal maidens,/[12] yet may I be permitted

---

[12] As a mother and widow, Sapientia can never aspire to the highest heavenly honors. She has

to join them in their eternal praise of Thee, who art not the Father,/ but art of the same substance with the Father/ and the Holy Ghost, sole Lord of the Universe, sole King of the upper, mid and lower regions, Thou who reignest and art Lord forever and ever.

Matrons: Receive her, O Lord, Amen.

hopes, however, of becoming the "mother-in-law" of Christ. Cf. Saint Jerome, *Epistola ad Eustochium*, 22, 20 (Sapientia refers to herself as *socrus* in *Sapientia*, IV, 3).

Saint John[1]

I

The virgin John saw the heavens open
And beheld the Father of all on His resplendent throne,
Surrounded by a row of twice twelve elders
Who glittered with gleaming crowns,
All dressed in robes of gleaming white;
He also saw at the enthroned King's right hand
A book, whose secret no man can learn.

II

This angel here, seeking a worthy man, finds none
Who could solve the seal of the secret book.

III

He consoles John, who is weeping
As he explains that the Lamb can solve the seals.

IV

Behold, the secrets of the book lay open for the slain Lamb
Whose praise Heavens' citizens soon sing;
Behold Faith's martyrs, bearing witness near the altar with clear voices.
They receive robes glittering with gleaming whiteness.
The angel, arriving from the direction of rosy sunrise,
Marks the Eternal King's servants on their foreheads.

---

1   These 35 hexameters follow the dramas in the Emmeram codex. It has been suggested that
they were used as *tituli* to a series pictures depicting scenes from the Apocalypse (see
Homeyer, *Opera*, p. 376). For a discussion of the poem, see Edwin Zeydel, "On the Two
Minor Poems in the Hrotsvitha Codes," *Modern Language Notes* 60 (1945): 373–76. Peter
Dronke, *Women Writers*, p. 63, asks: "Or is it possible that the apocalyptic verses *were*
performed? In principle there is nothing implausible about this. From the decade 965–75 –
a time when Hrotsvitha was at the height of her powers – we have the first surviving detailed
instructions, set down at Winchester, about how the resurrection ceremony, *Quem Queritis*,
should be mimed."

Afterwards John beheld many standing there in white,
Praising the Lamb, and carrying palm leaves in hand.
Behold, Heaven's citizens are silent for half an hour.
He stood at the sacred altar with a censer
And carried incense, symbolizing the faithfuls' holy prayers.

V

Behold, a woman glitters, surrounded by the splendid sun,
Adorned with a gleaming crown of twice twelve stars.
A snake wants to devour her tender young son,
But the dragon has fallen from Heaven and is cast to the earth.
Behold the Lamb standing here on the Mount of Zion,
And the company of virgins singing new songs.
The beast attacks the saints with all the dragon's might;
But truth has laid him low; arriving on a white steed,
He whips the ancient snake to savage Tartarus.
Behold, the books of life are held open to the dead
And, alive, they rise, freed from the chains of death.
Soon all receive their due according to their merits.

Gesta Oddonis[1]

When the King of Kings,   who alone reigns forever
And who governs the length and succession   of all kings' reigns on earth,
Ordained that supreme power   over the Frankish nation
Be passed on in succession   to the famous Saxon tribe
Whose name derives from rock,   strong as the Saxon's conviction,
Then that power passed on   to Duke Otto's son,
By the name of Henry;   as king he ruled the land,
Pious and just he ruled   as he carried the sceptre.
My greatly flawed poem   will never succeed, I know,
To depict adequately   the breadth of his noble excellence,
Or how benevolently he reigned   over all the conquered nations,
Or how he surpassed in virtue   so many kings on earth.
Firm always with the wicked,   kind always to the good,
He observed the land's laws   to the smallest detail,
And rewarded all his people   according to their merits.
Then the Lord God Christ,   Lord of peace in Heaven,
Granted perpetual peace   as long as Henry reigned.
Happy were the years,   when he, at the kingdom's summit
Spent, if I'm not mistaken,   sixteen years in peace.
His wife ruled with him;   famous far and wide,
No woman in the kingdom   could ever compare to her.
No one could surpass her   in her mighty merits.
God bestowed upon them   the gift of three male offspring.
With zealous care providing   for the happy nation
So that after Henry's death,   whom every landsman honored,
Usurpers could not seize   the royal crown with force,
But that the royal sons   of the reigning family
Would rule their father's kingdom   in harmony and peace.
Though each was awarded   a position of great honor
The two younger brothers   served the oldest who reigned.
Otto, the first born,   shone forth among them
Like the morning star, glittering,   in the aura of perfection.
Him chose God Almighty in   prudent anticipation

---

[1]   The *Gesta* was composed before October 11, 965, the date of the death of Archbishop Bruno
of Cologne, who is mentioned in the epic as still living.

To be the protector   of this Christian nation:
Oldest he was in years,   and greatest in his merits,
As duly befits him   who inherits the crown.
It would need far more   than a few simple words
To praise the youth's virtue,   his exemplary nature;
Christ distinguished him now   with extraordinary honors
As He bestowed upon him   the high rule over Rome,
Which has always been   the earth's proud capital.
With Christ's help he succeeded   to hold the barbarians at bay,
Who earlier tore apart   our holy mother Church often.
He was followed in age   by his brother Henry,
Gloriously named so   for his famous father.
Christ's wise care provided   that he serve his nation
As a firm and good leader   and protect the Church.
Bellicose, and manly,   versed in war and weapons,
His courage like a boulder,   boldly resisting the enemies' assault.
The third son was then born,   Bruno, the Church's pillar;
The eternal priest's mercy   deemed him fully worthy
To be the protector   of all catholic people.
His earthly father, therefore,   on divine suggestion,
Persuaded him to vow   his life to Christ's service.
Early he took the child   from his loving mother
And had him renounce   the royal court's pomp
To become Christ's soldier,   king of the star-clad tent.
The eternal Father's true wisdom   showed Himself generous
And kind to this vassal.   He gave Bruno such gifts of the mind
That none could compare   with him in deep learning
None among the wise   in this our perishable world.
As the boys grew up,   trained in courtly manner
The king, their illustrious father,   still in quite good health
And breathing the vigor   of his noble life's breath,
Decided to choose   a worthy wife for Otto,
His first begotten son,   and heir to his throne,
A wife truly worthy   of such an exalted union.

Yet he sought her not   on the native soil,
But he sent messengers,   trusty and courteous,
Across the wide sea,   to the worthy isle of Anglos.
These were instructed   to woo with many gifts,
For Edith, daughter of Edward   the noble English king.
She had remained at court   after her father's death
While her brother carried   the scepter as king.

A woman of humble birth   bore the son to the king
Edith, however, was   the king's noble wife's child,
While the brother's mother   came not of noble stock.
This lovely young virgin   of whom these verses tell
Enjoyed early on   a stellar reputation.
Of noble descent she was,   endowed with special gifts,
And counted mighty kings   among her fine ancestors.
Her noble countenance   shone forth in stellar beauty,
Wondrously reflecting   her worthy family line.
Because of perfection   in her traits and manners,
She was so highly praised   in her native country,
That in the unanimous   judgment of the people
She was held the highest   among all the women.
No one, though, will marvel   at her great perfection,
Knowing that her ancestors   included even saints.
For it is told that Edith   descended from Oswald,
That famous king whose glory   is still sung far and wide,
For he sacrificed his life   for the glory of Christ Jesus.

As the king's messengers   appeared at the palace
Before the virgin's brother,   residing there at court,
They promptly revealed to him   their secret mission.
Their message prompted   enthusiastic support.
Soon he revealed the news   cautiously to his sister
And urged her to accept   the Christian king's proposal
Who sought her as a bride   for his own dear son.
The brother's admonition,   clothed in friendly words,
Soon inspired deep love   in her for the youth.
Then, eagerly, the brother   collected great treasures.
And when he concluded   to have gathered enough
He gave his dear sister   a proper train of servants
To attend to the lady   on her voyage abroad.
He also provided her   with many costly treasures
And sent along her sister,   Adiva, too, with her,[2]
Who was younger in years   and, thus, lesser in merits.
In order to show   most distinguished honors
To the illustrious son   of the celebrated king,

---

[2] Hrotsvit is the only contemporary historian to record that Edith arrived at the Saxon court
accompanied by her sister. Perhaps as a woman, and a privileged observer of court matters,
Hrotsvit knew of the potential plight of foreign brides bereft of kin, and wanted to stress this
alleviating circumstance of Edith's arrival.

He sent him two virgins   of great and noble descent.
Edith conquered all   even at first sight
Rightfully so because   of her perfect nature;
She was proclaimed worthy   of the royal offspring.
This illustrious wife   soon bore him a fine son.
He was named Liudolf;   brought honor to his parents.
All people of the nation   loved him most tenderly,
And wished most heartily   that his life would last long.
As all this was happening,   King Henry's death approached.
The entire nation   deeply mourned his death,
All who, justly ruled,   lived under his reign.
Then the kingdom's rule   was taken over by Otto,
King Henry's eldest son,   his much admired heir.
He was elected unanimously   by all tribes of the land,
And was anointed king   with men's and Christ's approval.
God's heavenly mercy   gave him such rich gifts
That he was rightly praised   by all for his merits.
He surpassed many kings   whose lands the oceans lick.
Also, God's holy hand   protected him from harm
From the enemy's plots   and also from their guiles;
One could almost think   that faithful David ruled,[3]
Renewing, once again,   the glory of his deeds.

Mildly Otto ruled   not only those people
Who had bowed their necks   under his father's rule before.
No, he also conquered   many pagan tribes
Whom he then made subject   to the soldiers of Christ
In order to strengthen   the peace of holy Church.
Regardless of how often   he rode forth in battle
Never did his foes win,   no matter how brave,
Never could they wound him   or gain victory in battle
Protected as he was   by the heavenly King's hand.
His army never succumbed   to the weapons of his foe,
Except, perhaps, at times   when men went to battle
Against the king's orders   on forbidden land.

Henry, the king's brother   was the realm's first duke,
Enjoying lasting peace   still back in those days;
Men gave him his due   right respect and honor.

---

3   On the Otto-David analogies, see Dennis Kratz, "The Nun's Epic: Hrotswitha on Christian
Heroism," in *Wege der Worte*, ed. D.C. Riechel (Cologne, Vienna, 1978), pp. 132–42.

He wed a worthy bride   of noble ancestry
Daughter of Duke Arnulf   by the name of Judith.
She was a fine woman   of surpassing beauty
And, what's more important,   one of perfect virtue.
As all this occurred,   calm peace ruled the realm
Even if for limited time,   as the people wished.
In those blessed days   the weapons were still silent.
Oh, what perfect bliss,   what blessed, glorious times,
What magnificent gifts   bestowed upon the land,
Those years could have been   under our wise king's rule,
Had not the wicked guile   of the ancient serpent
Undermined our peace   by insidious deceit!
When the foreign nations   had all been defeated,
Inner conflict rose   suddenly at home.
Civil wars then raged   and tore the land apart,
Inflicting more harm   than frequent wars with neighbors.
Not insignificant was   the reason for this evil:
A fervent quarrel flared up   between the realm's great men.
One faction chose to follow   the king's own brother Henry,
Ready to do his bidding   in every possible way,
While another chose to follow   the lead of Count Eberhard.
Both sides swore allegiance   to their respective leaders,
Aggravating thereby   the conflict more severely
As the conflict sharpened,   as I said before,
The count I just mentioned   succeeded in attaining
Castle Baduliki   with mercenaries' help,
Who, covered by night's dark,   fell upon the castle.
He dragged off poor Duke Henry,   the king's noble brother
And took him as prisoner.   The duke's snow-white hands,
Usually all bedecked   with bejeweled rings,
Were now most cruelly   bound up in fetters.
Savagely he scattered   Henry's splendid treasures;
And also abducted   his king's only son,
In order to use him   as an ally in battle.
When the king learned of this,   he mourned most bitterly,
And weeping he bemoaned   the miserable deed.
Not willing to tolerate   his brother's great suffering,
He followed the example   of Patriarch Abraham,
Who, pitying Loth,   rescued him from harm.
Soon he succeeded   in collecting an army,
A more than modest crowd   from all corners of the country
Then in regal pomp   he set forth, determined,

To succor his poor brother,   suffering great pain.
Without any delay   he set free his brother
And passed judgment on those   who committed the crime.
Some he punished with death   to hang at the gallows.
And others he banished   from their dear homes.
The strife no sooner ended,   resolved by the king's wisdom,
When the ancient deceiver   and enemy of all
Once again conspired   to a new, more heinous crime,
So evil that it'll serve   as a warning to all ages.
For when this Eberhard   returned from banishment
And in his cherished home   once again he dwelled –
His return was granted   by the good king's grace –
Then be persuaded Gislberth,   tied to him in friendship
(An act that for sure,   couldn't please you, Christ!),
To take the just king captive,   Otto, God's anointed,
And thus to deprive him   of his due regal rights
By means of an unjust act   against the just monarch.
They also made Henry   the faithful king's brother
Party to this plan,   evilly conceived,
Persuading him in secret   with honeyed words and flattery
Not to requite the wrong   he previously had suffered,
But to show himself receptive   to their insidious wishes
And yearn to seize the crown   ousting his brother.
He, conquered finally   by their flattering speeches,
Promised (oh what sorrow),   to comply with their plan;
He even pledged his promise   by a solemn, binding oath;
But for sure it can't be   that he thought this in his heart,
I trust he probably gave   his word under duress.
Those misfits, who were swayed   by vain, vacuous hopes,
Believed they could bring him,   who ruled over the people
Soon under the yoke   of their own weak rule.
But the King of Heaven,   the orb's most equitable judge,
He who alone knows   men's every secret thought
And who alone can deal   with a mortal heart's craze,
Shattered with His right,   the hand that created all,
Also these men's plan   of the enormous crime.
He turned the evil plan   onto the plan's conceivers,
On them who planned to harm   Otto, Christ's anointed.
They, who prepared the traps   for their own rightful lord,
Were, themselves, captured   in their own insidious traps.
I must not presume here   to have sufficient talent
That I could hope to sing   and depict in well-turned phrases

With what marvelous mercy   Christ's heavenly grace
Showered unceasingly   on our justly blessed king,
How often He saved him   from the many traps
That the insidious foe   prepared for him with guile;
But it is not decorous   for a fragile woman
Residing in the folds   of a cloister's quiet,
To tell the tale of warfare,   of which she does not know.
That has always been   the task of learned men
Who, in their wisdom   and their grave intellect,
Describe everything   in their polished letters,
And relate what happened   from beginning to end.
I will only tell this   (because that's all I can tell):
He who alone can work   wondrous miracles,
He who rescued David   from the guiles of Saul
And gave him the scepter   so that he may rule,
He likewise protected   our king who followed
David's just example   in piety and virtue,
And repeatedly saved him   from thousandfold danger.

Primordia

The Origins of the Gandersheim Abbey

Behold, the deep devotion   of my humble mind
Is eager to sing   and tell of the founding
Of our great cloister,   the Gandersheim Abbey,
Built with no small efforts,   and care by Saxon dukes,
Mighty leaders by right: Liudulf the great lord
And also his son Oddo   who completed the task.[1]

The necessary order   of all such things demands it
That first the construction   of the famous cloister
Be depicted aptly   in our song as due.
Inception of its building   was ordered by Liudulf
Duke of great Saxony,   reverent in spirit.
He, born of noble stock   and illustrious parentage,
Proved himself worthy   of his great family
In his noble conduct   and his deeds of virtue.
Among all the Saxons   he was deemed most worthy.
Liudulf was thoughtful   and also very handsome,
Prudent in his speeches,   and cautious in his actions,
In him was placed the hope   and glory of his tribe.
Therefore he was summoned   to serve in Louis' army,
Louis the great king   of the Frankish nation,
By whom he was soon raised   rightly to great honors.
Receiving his countdom   as leader of the Saxons,
Becoming princes' equal,   not unlike to dukes,
He surpassed in virtue   all of his forefathers
And surpassed them no less   in rank and in honors.
He had married Oda,   a lady of high birth

---

[1] The *Primordia* was composed during Otto II's reign (973–83) after the great fire of 970 which destroyed the Gandersheim church. Rather than emphasizing the salvific efficacy of the relics of Saints Anastasius and Innocent, brought back from Rome by Liudolf and Oda, Hrotsvit chooses to stress the patronage of the Liudolf clan by linking past and present through the continued leadership of Liudolf abbesses, the buried remains there of the Liudolf ancestors, and their presentation throughout the epic as agents of divine providence.

From a famed family   of noble, mighty Franks.
She was Billung's daughter   the worthy, noble prince,
And of famous Aeda,   generous, good lady.
Aeda had devoted   her whole life completely
To serving God almighty   and to frequent prayers.
For her firm devotion   borne out in pious deeds,
She was well rewarded   and told of heaven's plans
When John was sent to her,   John who baptized Christ,
To reveal the future   and tell how her descendants
Would, in years, proceed   to Imperial glory.

Once when Aurora   with her splendid light rays
Had already parted   the dark shadow of night
She, as was her wont   lay prostrate, all alone,
Before the sacred altar   consecrated to John,
And battered heaven's gates   with incessant prayers.
As she was occupied   in these worthy efforts
She noticed a man's feet   standing close to her.
Quite disturbed, she wondered   who the man might be.
Who would dare presume   to disturb her quiet
And interrupt her time   devoted to deep prayer?
Lifting up her head   and turning around slightly,
She beheld a young man   in glittering splendor
Wrapped in a rough garment   of yellowish color
Appearing, as it were,   woven from camel's hair.
The whiteness of his face,   radiant with beauty,
Was graced by a small beard   of the very same hue
As his lovely hair: all black and shiny.
Aeda, beholding him,   knew he wasn't mortal.
She grew very frightened   as is women's wont;
Then greatly terrified,   she fell to the ground.
He, however, spoke,   with kind words reassuring
The trembling lady thus: "Fear you not, but conquer
Your fear and terror.   Set aside your worry
And know now who I am: I am that self same John
Who once was found worthy   to baptize the Lord Jesus
In the river's waves.   And since you so cherish me
I bring you joyful tidings: your famed descendants
Will found a cloister   to house holy virgins,
And while they remain steadfast   and firm in their devotion
Peace and calm will reign   and good cheer in the land.
Your own descendants   will, too, in future years

Shine forth in such glory   and at such heights of honor
That no other kingdoms   will compare with theirs
In might and in power   in that particular epoch."
He spoke thus and promptly   returned to higher ether
Leaving this sweet solace   with the blessed lady.

Interpretive Essay

Genre

All of Hrotsvit's works are generic hybrids. All belong – to one degree or another – to the realm of hagiography. In all the saint and/or the virtuous person becomes the re-presentation of Christ and the mimetic paradigm of Christian virtue which sets a model articulating, in Hawley's phrase, "Christianity's highest sense of itself."[1] As literal as well as symbolic truth "the sacred *vita* lent itself perfectly for genre mixing" since as a direct instrument for religious and moral didacticism it was bound to utilize diverse genres for their recognized mimetic, didactic, or aesthetic functions.

The predilection for the hybridization of genres was, according to Alastair Fowler, especially prominent in the Middle Ages, nowhere more obviously, perhaps, than in hagiographic texts where modal transformations were mandated by the ontological privileging of extra literary concerns.[2] The privileging of aesthetic criteria over moral and pedagogical values in judging the merits of the written word would have been as alien to the early medieval reader/writer as was the concept of pure classical genres. As Alastair Fowler observes,

> They [medieval genres] may be classical, or classical misunderstood, or classical reinterpreted, or vernacular equivalent, or vernacular oblivious, or vernacular artful and innovative. However, as the existence of fairly sophisticated epistolary rhetoric shows, all this is not to be put down to mere incapacity – still less to disregard for genre. We have to look for explanations of the disorder, first in the practical aims of the grammarians, and second in the difficulties that emergent forms present to the genre critic.[3]

Since it has been Hrotsvit's dramas (rather than her legends or epics) that have initiated the authenticity debate and have become the most widely read texts of the *corpus*, I would like to concentrate on exploring the confluence of two generic modes (the hagiographic and the dramatic) converging on their potential for mimesis in her dramas. It is my conten-

---

[1] Hawley, *Saints and Virtue* (Berkeley, 1987), pp. xv–xvi.
[2] Alastair Fowler, *Kinds of Literature* (Cambridge, 1982).
[3] *Ibid.*, p. 146.

tion that Hrotsvit, I believe, composed her hagiographic lessons in a hybrid dramatic form for reasons practical, theoretical, and aesthetic. She chose to graft a pedagogically valuable and morally superior mimetic form, the sacred *vita* (which not only intended to manifest the continuing nature of divine grace or Church dogma but also mandated – by insistence on author-reader interaction – an adherence to and emulation of the ideal promoted), onto a pragmatically mimetic, aesthetically superior, but morally valueless form, Terentian comedy (which not only claimed to be a *simulacrum* of life but was accused by the early Church fathers of inciting improper action by claiming divine precedence for human frailty and by centering its concerns squarely on the human, the facile and temptingly easy pursuit of happiness). She gave her readers what they needed to read in a form they wanted to read. Drama was prohibited and repeatedly castigated by the Church for its mimetic power, although Terence was read in schools because of his eloquence; sacred biography, conversely, was advocated and promoted by the Church as a powerful tool of teaching and preaching because of its mimetic potential, since the life of the saint functioned as a mimetic paradigm; aesthetically, however, hagiographic texts ranged from the marginally literate and clumsily simplistic examples of the early Middle Ages to the ornate and eloquent compilations of the eleventh and twelfth centuries. Hrotsvit, then, attempted a perfectly logical and masterfully conceived fusion of two mimetically defined genres by grafting her hagiographic plots and liturgical prayers onto the Terentian form.

According to Thomas Heffernan, sacred biography transcends history because "the essential thing being signified (the presence of the divine in the saint) exists outside a system where sign and signified can be empirically validated."[4] Sacred narratology thus conflates heavenly and earthly ontologies and evokes "the meaning which erupts when these two ontological planes collide."[5]

The Middle Ages were teeming with various forms of hagiographic texts. The *Biblioteca Hagiographia Latina* alone contains over nine thousand *vitae*. They vary in style, length, complexity, linguistic polish, genre, and mode. Saint Augustine's pronouncement offered hagiographers creative license in their composition by extending to them a system which was equipped for symbolic as well as literalist representation, for Augustine held that eloquence without wisdom was empty, but wisdom without eloquence also had limited use. Language, therefore, had to be utilized accordingly to convey the reality demanded by the situation. This

4   Thomas Heffernan, *Sacred Biography* (New York, 1988), p. 9.
5   *Ibid.*, p. 11.

flexibility is usually seen as inherently "anti-sophist" for its insistence, as Thomas Heffernan argues, that the *res* or dialectic of an argument was more critical than *eloquentia*. While this hierarchy was widely accepted in the Middle Ages, it was by no means categorical. For instance, the *Glossa Ordinaria*, in glossing the parable of the talents, equates the bad servant and his single coin with an *intellectus* deprived of his eloquence. Eloquence, on the other hand, is associated with the second servant's duplication of the two talents interpreted as the preaching of the word by using *figura* and *exempla*.[6]

Heffernan's assessment of this distinction's importance to hagiography in general and to the medieval proclivity for hybridization in specific is crucial for an understanding of the practice of medieval genre mixing:

> what is of fundamental importance for this view of narrative in sacred biography is the idea that language is syncretistic; it cannot only harmonize different ontological planes, heaven and earth, but, if necessary, it can also contradict its own required structures to do so.[7]

There is no question as to the hagiographic nature of Hrotsvit's plots nor her privileging the *res* of her themes over the *eloquentia* of her model but there is also no question of her wish to clothe her "wisdom" in elegant garb. Her sources for the dramas are well known and her *apologia* for using the Terentian form often discussed. Lesser known, however, are her methodology of composition and her liturgical and especially doxological framing devices for the plays that serve, I believe, as the critical *nexus* to the services, especially the sermons, and as the diacritical marks framing her attempts to harmonize the vastly divergent ontological planes of Christian instruction with pagan theater, revelatory history and symbolic presentation with the verisimilitude of dialogic presentation.

The structural elements of Hrotsvit's texts bearing obvious associations with the liturgy are the doxological formulas concluding most of her works.[8] The formulas that conclude the individual dramas fall into two classes. One class consists of Trinitarian formulas ("qui regnat et gloriatur in unitate trinitatis. Amen," *Gallicanus*, XIII, 7 for instance), and the other formulas list glorifying attributes ("Ipsi soli honor, virtus, fortitudo et victoria, laus et iubilatio per infinita saeculorum saecula. Amen," *Calimachus*, IX, 33). *Gallicanus*, *Paphnutius*, and *Sapientia* have formu-

---

6   *Patrologia Latina*, vol. 114, col. 165.
7   Heffernan, *Sacred Biography*, p. 9.
8   For a full discussion of the liturgical elements in Hrotsvit's works, see Jonathan Black, "The Use of Liturgical Texts in Hrotsvit's Works," in *Hrotsvit of Gandersheim, "Rara Avis in Saxonia"* (Ann Arbor, 1987), pp. 165–82.

las belonging to the first class; *Dulcitius*, *Calimachus*, and *Abraham* have formulas of the second.

The first type is modeled after the standard doxological formulas used after each collect in the Mass and Office.[9] The second type is also used in the liturgy (e.g. "Benedictio . . . honor, virtus et fortitudo Deo nostro in saecula saeculorum," Antiphon, trinity, CAO III, 1710). Hrotsvit's utilization of these two different types of liturgical formulas in framing her hagiographic texts is not in itself unusual especially if we look upon the dramas as thematic double-takes of the legends in different form. What *is* notable is the effect of the formulas on the positioning of the dramas as sacred narratology squarely into the pulpit or the refectory as well as their role in reminding their audiences of the metatexts for the plays: the Roman Benedictine Liturgy and the Benedictine liturgical calendar.

The third constituent element of the Hrotsvithean hybrid texts is drama. Hrotsvit's conformity to the general definitions of drama by late Roman and early medieval theorists and grammarians is quite obvious.[10] They all define drama as dialogue and as a narrative beginning in turbulence and ending in tranquility. In fact, Evanthius's definition is still felt as late as in Dante's letter to Can Grande emphasizing comedy's gradual move away from worldliness. I have argued elsewhere and in great detail Hrotsvit's close adherence to the formal precept of Terentian comedy advocated by Evanthius; let it suffice to say here that she follows closely the rules established and promoted by him.

While Hrotsvit follows the formal precepts of drama as described and praised by Evanthius, her plays conform only partially to his thematic definition of comedy; she borrows what suits her hagiographic plots and transmutes or omits what does not.

> Inter tragoediam autem et comoediam cum multa tum inprimis hoc distat, quod in comoedia mediocres fortunae hominum, parvi impetus periculorum laetique sunt exitus actionum, at in tragoedia omnia contra . . . : *et illic prima turbulenta, tranquilla ultima*, in tragoedia contrario ordine res aguntur; tum quod in tragoedia fugienda vita, in comoedia capessenda exprimitur; postremo quod omnis comoedia de fictis est argumentis, tragoedia saepe de historia fide petitur.[11]

---

9 Liturgical books characteristically include only the incipit ("Per," "Qui vivis") as in the case in *Gallicanus*, II: "praestare domino nostro Iesu Christo, qui vivit" (IX, 2).

10 For a full discussion of Hrotsvit's adherence to the general precepts, see K. Wilson, *Hrotsvit of Gandersheim: The Ethics of Authorial Stance* (Leiden: Brill, 1988).

11 Evanthius, in *Donatus commentum Terenti*, ed. P. Wessner, Bibliotheca Scriptorum Graecorum et Romanorum Teubneriana (Stuttgart: Teubner, 1962), vol. 1, p. 21.

(Between tragedy and comedy there is, among others, this dif-
ference: that in comedy men of middle fortunes are depicted, as
are small dangers, and a happy ending, while in tragedy the
opposites occur. In comedy disturbance comes first but tranquility at the end, in tragedy, the exact reversal of that order. In
tragedy [the depiction] of life is to be shunned, in comedy,
followed. Finally, the arguments presented in comedy are all
based on fiction, but in tragedy, on truth.)

Clearly, the definitions are given in terms of subject matter (*res*) – an
aspect of drama Hrotsvit admittedly wishes to counteract. Her dramas,
she says, are only Terentian in form, but as to their subject matter she
vows to present the inversion of the pagan poet's themes: for lascivious
women engaged in illicit passion in Terence's comedies, she says, she will
substitute saintly and virginal women triumphing over the temptations of
the flesh; for corrupting pastime she will substitute useful Christian
instruction – assertions which earned Hrotsvit's plays the description
"anti-Terenz." Because of the superimposition of the hagiographic *res*
over the Terentian *eloquentia* inversion is precisely what happens to
Evanthius's stratification of comic subject matter. Since Hrotsvit upholds
an ideal to be emulated rather than, like Terence, entertaining his audience
by comedies of manners representative of his contemporaries, her heroines are seldom *mediocres fortunate*: they face more than *parvi impetus
periculorum*, as the plays' torture-scenes and grave temptations attest;
while the outcomes of the plays do bring eternal life and celestial rewards
to the protagonists, they inevitably suffer martyrdom; while they do desire
eternal life, they flee life on earth; and, finally, her dramas, she insists,
relate truth and not fiction.

Evanthius's insistence that "in tragedy the kind of life is shown that
is to be shunned; while in comedy the kind is shown that is to be followed"
is fully borne out in Hrotsvit's statements of dramatic purpose. Similarly,
regarding the didactic intent of comedy and the tremendously mimetic
appeal of the theater, Hrotsvit is in full accordance with Evanthius – she
only wishes to teach something entirely different and to teach it differ-
ently: not only by negative but also by positive example. Evanthius quotes
Cicero on comedy, "comoediam esse cicero ait imitationem vitae, speculum consuetudinis, imaginem veritatis,"[12] Hrotsvit, too, defines the poetic aim of her dramas in didactic terms; she, however, wishes to uphold
a mirror of laudable excellence to which the reader is to rise through
emulation.

---

[12] *Ibid.*, p. 23.

Hrotsvit's specific reasons for drawing on Terentian drama are not apologistic but aesthetic/poetological: they concern the *amplificatio*, the revitalization of her hagiographic themes presented earlier in the eight legends by the infusion of "new" poetological considerations in the form of an innovative hybridized genre. She wished to use the Terentian form because he was read and enjoyed, and she wished to provide a substitute for that reading and enjoying. He offered her a formal model that, *mutatis mutandis*, gave her an opportunity to present her Christian heroines for the glory of God and the edification and salvation of his creatures. This is a subversive mimesis, which attempts to expose the falsity of what it adopts and interiorizes by substituting good for evil in the very same form of expression. The rhetorical concept for this process of hybridization, imitation as critique to discredit the opponent, is set forth by Quintilian, who advocates the imitation of the adversary as an effective rhetorical strategy for discrediting him. Hrotsvit's strategy is homeopathic, that is, healing by the application of pathogenic agents: to cure *similia similibus*.

In the preface to her dramas Hrotsvit states her authorial intentions:

> There are many Catholics and we cannot entirely acquit our-
> selves of this accusation, who prefer the vanity of pagan books
> on account of the elegance of their style, to the usefulness of
> sacred scripture. There are also others, who, devoted to sacred
> writings and spurning pagan works, yet read the (*figmenta*)
> fantastic fiction of Terence frequently, and while they delight in
> the sweetness of his style, they are stained by the knowledge of
> [exposure to] wicked events. Wherefore I, the Strong Voice of
> Gandersheim, did not refuse to imitate in composition him whom
> other are accustomed to read, so that in the same form of writing
> in which the shameless acts of lascivious women have been
> depicted the laudable chastity of Christian women may be cele-
> brated according to the ability of my poor talent. (*Opera*, p. 235)

Her program is developed in three sets of interlocking antitheses: pagan uselessness vs. Christian utility, sweetness of style vs. moral perdition in subject matter, and most importantly, lies vs. truth. Hrotsvit's anger at Terence prompts her response. Her reference to Terence's noxious *figmenta* stands in marked contrast to her own repeated attestations of useful *veritas*, or hagiographic truth, as the source and theme of her works, reflecting in this way her triple purpose: first, she contrasts helpful Christian truths with dangerous pagan lies; secondly, she substitutes chaste Christian women for the pagan poet's lascivious courtesans, thus creating female characters who exemplify traits worthy of emulation; thirdly, she creates Christian alter- or antiplays intended to supplant pagan comedy, at least for her limited audience. This is clearly an exercise in one-upmanship empowered by the doctrinal superiority of her subject matter, and by her "scholarly" approach to appropriating the genre. In this manner hagiographic truth is conveyed through the depiction of feminine excellence and the glorious triumph of Christianity over paganism is achieved through the victory of faithful, determined and chaste Christian women over amorous, weak and evil pagan men. Her poetic manifesto is subtle. While in the preface to her legends she conforms to the traditional gynocentric concept of the female monastic author as a divinely authorized instrument of God's ongoing revelation by referring to herself, like Hildegard of Bingen and other early female religious writers, as a musical instrument played by the Divine player, in the preface to her plays she does not. Neither does she follow her authorial identification – as Hildegard and Julian do – with repeating the traditional theme of God's choosing feeble women in order to confound mighty men thus endorsing the notion of women's self-evident lack of authority *qua* creationally subordinate females which is counteracted by God's redemptive empowerment. Rather, in a stroke of rhetorical genius, she herself transfers that redemptive empowerment to her heroines who, frail though they might be, will confound mighty men. This authorial empowerment by its clear analogy to the redemptive topos firmly legitimizes her exemplary constructs within the cohesively androcentric boundaries of tenth century monasticism.

In the preface to the dramas Hrotsvit objects to the depiction of the "shameless acts of lascivious women" ("turpia lasciviarum incesta feminarum") for which she wishes to substitute the laudable chastity of holy virgins. This may come as quite a surprise to one reading Terence, for as K. de Luca observes, the Roman poet's depravity is greatly overstated.[13] In fact the Terentian characters' moral wickedness – or even sexual appetite – pales in comparison to that of Hrotsvit's (male) protagonists engaging – or attempting to engage – in diverse sexual aberration from multiple fornication to necrophilia.

Hrotsvit's indignation against Terence, though, springs not necessarily from reading his plays but from the long tradition of Christian invective against the theater, notably the treatises of Tertullian and Augustine. Tertullian and Augustine inveigh against the sexual mores depicted in and inspired by Roman comedy corrupting by condoning and delighting in carnal sin while, at the same time, the divine is dragged down into the mire of human sexuality. The most subversive element of Terence's drama for Hrotsvit must have been the devaluation of the divine at the aggran-

---

13 Kenneth de Luca, "Hrotsvit's 'Imitation' of Terence," *Classical Folia* 28 (1974): 90.

dizement of the human; the total ontological inversion of sacred narratology where the presence of the divine in the saint imparts the seminal meaning to the plot. The true center of existence in Terence's plays is man; a universe which for Hrotsvit, as it was for Tertullian and Augustine, was devoid of meaning because it was a world with its center totally misplaced. Terence's *humanitas* only has a place at the margins of her world occupied by its rightful center of *divinitas*. This is not to say that Terentian comedy has always maintained (or considered) itself as pure classical form, as uncontaminated genre. It, too, is a hybrid.

Terence, in fact, promises his audience something borrowed and something new, the presentation of Greek New comedy in Roman garb, whereby he carefully distinguishes between plot, thought, and style (or content, presentation, and expression respectively). In the prologue to the *Andria* he says: "ita non sunt dissimili argumento sed tamen dissimili oratione sunt fictae et stilo." What he takes from the Greeks is the plot and certain stock characters and, needless to say, the form; presentation, psychology, and style are his own. He admits to the practice of *contaminatio* regarding his use of Greek plots, and justifies his use of *imitatio* concerning his occasional stylistic and verbal borrowing from talented men by presenting them as worthy of imitation. Hrotsvit, on the other hand, apologizes for her use of formal *imitatio* but takes pride in presenting subject matter and characters diametrically opposed to those of Terence. What she imitates is the *genus dictationis* (that is, the generic form of what she believed the dramatic rules of comedy would require). In terms of style and expression (*dictatio, sententiae*) she knows herself to be inferior to her model; in her source of inspiration, her subject matter and her themes, on the other hand, she sees herself as Terence's superior. What she presents is truth, what she teaches are the precepts of divine revellation, what she upholds is the Christian ascetic ideal. Fortified with the weapons of hagiography, she can battle Terence; fortified with his form of presentation, she intends to lure her readers from pagan drama to sacred *vita*, from Terence's preoccupation with *humanitas* to the proper Christian concern for *divinitas*. And in the process she creates a hybrid form which is neither classical comedy nor sacred legend but embryonic Christian drama paving the way, at least in principle if not in practice, for the mystery and miracle plays of the later Middle Ages.

Hrotsvit's Humor

Far from simplistic, Hrotsvit's humor is a cornucopia of multifaceted and often quite sophisticated instances of self-conscious textual complexities. As an interplay between audience/reader and text/author, access to her humor is predicated on the reader's awareness of the metatext (her audience's cultural, liturgical, biblical, and hagiographic glossing of the legends', epics' and plays' action). Comic elements range from bawdy scatology, such as the involuntary fart that Gongolf's wife sends forth every time she opens her mouth as a punishment for her refusal to repent and recognize her dead husband's sanctity (a marvelous inversion of the heroic eloquence of Hrotsvit's virginal martyrs), to voyeurism, when the three young innocent virgins in *Dulcitius* are glued to the key hole observing the captain making amorous overtures to the pots and the pans mistaking it for love-making with the girls, to complex interactions between the metatexts of Catholic liturgy, Christian iconography, the "classics" read in school, and the Hrotsvithean texts.

An excellent example for the latter is *The Resurrection of Drusiana and Calimachus*. As the play's title implies, this is a resurrection play, invoking the season of Lent, the temptation and passion of Christ, His descent to the underworld and His resurrection. It is not inconceivable that the arrangement and presentation/reading of the dramas echoed the liturgy stressing, thus, their applicatory, emulatory intention. In fact, I think it quite likely that the thematic double takes of the legends and the plays were intended as parallel construction to the Benedictine Office's practice of double analogical *lectiones* (for the Old and the New Testaments) followed by the sermon illustrating the morals through hagiographic examples. If that assumption is correct, then Hrotsvit would be anchoring the humor and sophisticated complexities of her plays' subtextual running commentary on monastic life and patristic ideology by drawing on her audience's cultural referents, that is to say their familiarity with the Church calendar, the Old and New Testaments, analogical logic as a way of glossing any text, the iconography of Scripture and hagiography and, of course, school authors such as Virgil, Terence and their commentators. Looking at *Calimachus* in this manner certainly enriches the reading experience of the work. The legend analogies to the play, *Basilius* and *Theophilus*, deal with temptation by the Devil, the succumbing of the (male) sinners to that temptation followed by two saintly (male) bishops' efforts to wrestle with Satan and wringing the repentant sinners' souls from him. They are, in other words, stories of epic struggles about spiritual death and resurrection, psychomachias of good and evil concretized in actual battles between Satan and the saintly representatives of the Church. In *Calimachus*, on the other hand, the protagonist is a woman (and a married woman at that), Drusiana, who is both the recipient of temptation and the catalyst of the sinner's conversion and salvation. Unlike the (male) protagonists of the legends, she not only does not succumb to temptation, but subsumes, in part, the salvific roles of the legends' male intercessors. As in other instances of Hrotsvit's sex inversion in her thematic double takes, so here too we see one-upmanship at work, and here, too, we see a female thwarting male power by refusing to allow herself to be the object of desire.

In light of the many metatextual undercurrents, the play's tomb-scene assumes a quagmirish complexity of association. As a passion analogy we see a heroic female's resistance to temptation, her death, resurrection, and subsequent magnanimity in forgiving those who trespassed against her. Unlike at Christ's grave, which was visited by the three Marys coming to anoint his limbs, the male visitors to Drusiana's tomb have a very different anointing in mind. Unlike the angel who guards Christ's tomb, Hrotsvit has the devilish Fortunatus at the entrance and, subsequently, the serpent coiled about the bodies. The serpent, of course, would evoke images of the Garden of Eden and of Lucifer in Hrotsvit's audience; it would, perhaps, also remind them of Virgil's Laokoon and his sons from Statius's commentary on Virgil's account of the Tale of Troy.[14] In the Statius commentary Laokoon's punishment is a result of his act of sacrilege (he and his wife desecrated Neptune's Temple by having sex in the sanctuary). Here too the crime is desecration in an erotic context, made even graver by the intent to commit that most heinous of sexual sins, necrophilia.

Hrotsvit's programatic statement in the preface to the dramas, "to show a frail Christian overcome strong men," is taken here, as elsewhere in the dramas, almost to the point of absurdity. When pursued by the handsome Calimachus (echoing, perhaps, the Greek love-poet's erotic reputation) Drusiana doesn't simply pray for strength to resist him nor for the standard hagiographic miracle of bodily change, not even for *his* departure or demise; no, she implores God to allow her to die to be able to forego temptation, and be the inspiration for another's sin. She thus subtly equates active and passive sinning, so perniciously linked by patristic writers, especially Tertullian, who invariably equate the objects of desire with desire itself. God promptly complies, and Drusiana dies. Calimachus, unlike the analogical legends' sinners, persists in his lust (to show Drusiana's stellar virtue, he has to be made a formidable adversary) and turns to necrophilia. In what might be one of Hrotsvit's most masterful instances of black humor, Calimachus delivers an ardently passionate address to the corpse after Fortunatus, having pocketed his bribe, praises the attractions of the still well preserved dead body. It is noteworthy that Calimachus, and Calimachus alone, this most monstrous of Hrotsvit's

---

14   On Dante's use of the same analogy, see Joseph Gibaldi and Richard LaFleur, "Vanni Fucci and Laocoon: Servius as Possible Intermediary Between Virgil and Dante," *Traditio* 32 (1976): 386–97.

erotic monsters, is the pagan youth whose initial speech echoes Augustine's (and subsequent Catholic writers') objections to the mimetic powers of festive comedy. Like Terence's young profligate referenced by suggestion, so Calimachus turns to the Gods to invoke divine precedent for his adulterous lust. Again, Hrotsvit's audience, aware perhaps of Europa's, Danae's, Semele's and Leda's helpless passivity, would, if not laugh, then certainly smile at Drusiana thwarting her ardent pursuer, and, by extension, at a frail and chaste Christian woman's victory over the gods of love.

The tomb scene is replete with analogical complexities. Aside from the initial "Lenten" approach by Calimachus, intent on bribing Fortunatus in order to gain access to Drusiana's body – a rather obscene burlesque of the three Marys visiting the tomb – we have another visitation with Pentecostal echoes by Andronicus, Drusiana's husband, and Saint John, their walk interrupted by divine intervention (the resurrected Christ) suggesting the events at the tomb and then voicing the injunction to glorify His name in the resurrected and consequently converted sinner. This missionary, Pentecostal injunction helps to explain the rather surprising turn of events at the tomb: Calimachus, not Drusiana, is revived first; this miracle is followed by a lengthy didactic dialogue of catechism during which the young man repents and embraces Christianity. Only after his function as missionary is concluded (with much verbose preachifying), does Saint John, at Andronicus's request, resurrect the heroine who, in yet one more instance of moral one-upmanship, begs for a second chance for Fortunatus who an hour or so earlier sold her body to Calimachus "to use as he pleased" (VII, 1). Fortunatus chooses to be dead rather than convert, ironically echoing thereby Hrotsvit's heroines' steadfastness in the face of pagan persecutions. The play concludes with a doctrinal lesson expounding the nature of free will and grace, glossing the events, and with a final jubilatory prayer to God.

Hrotsvit's humor, then, while subversive, is by no means radical. She does not supplant the patriarchal paradigm, she never questions the moral (ecclesiastical) hierarchy of virtues and virginity's place at their pinnacle; what she does is to appropriate and invert the paradigm, presenting a hierarchical system of her own in which the young and the female often reign and where the joy of religious devotion is practiced with a smile at the absurd and ludicrous inferiority of the foe and at the, perhaps, equally absurd and ludicrous tradition of patriarchal pretensions.

Select Bibliography

Editions

Bertini, Ferruccio, and Peter Dronke, ed. and trans. *Rosvita Dialoghi drammatici*. Milan: Garzanti, 1986.

Homeyer, Helena, ed. *Hrotsvithae Opera*. Munich, Paderborn, Vienna: Schöningh, 1970.

Pascal, Paul, ed. *Hrotsvitha: "Dulcitius" and "Paphnutius"*. Bryn Mawr Latin Commentaries. Bryn Mawr, 1985.

Strecker, Karl, ed. *Hrotsvithae Opera*. 2nd ed., Leipzig: Teubner, 1930.

Winterfeld, Paul von. *Hrotsvithae Opera*. Berlin: Weidmann, 1902.

Translations

Bonfante, Larissa, trans. *The Plays of Hrotsvitha von Gandersheim*. New York: New York Univeristy Press, 1979.

Homeyer, Helena, German trans. *Hrotsvitha von Gandersheim*. Munich, Paderborn, Vienna: Schöningh, 1973.

Piltz, Otto, German trans. *Die Dramen der Hroswitha von Gandersheim*. Leipzig: Reclam, 1925.

Wilson, Katharina. *The Plays of Hrotsvit of Gandersheim*. New York: Garland Press, 1989.

Critical Works

Aschbach, Joseph von. "Roswitha und Conrad Celtis." *Stiftungsberichte der philosophisch-historischen Klasse der Wissenschaften* 56 (1867): 3–62.

Batt, Michael. "Numerical Structure in Medieval Literature." *Formal Aspects of Medieval German Poetry*. Ed. S. Werbow. Austin: Univeristy of Texas Press, 1969, pp. 93–121.

Bauer, Albert, and Reinhold Rau, eds. *Quellen zur Geschichte der sächsischen Kaiserzeit*. Darmstadt: Wissenschaftliche Buchgesellschaft, 1971.

Bentner, Barbel. "Der Traum Abrahams." *Mittellateinisches Jahrbuch* 9 (1973): 22–30.

Bezold, F.V. "Konrad Celtis, 'der deutsche Erzhumanist?' " *Historische Zeitschrift* 49 (1883): 1–45; 193–228.

Bischoff, Bernhard. "Elementarunterricht und *Probationes Pennae* in der ersten Hälfte des Mittelalters." *Mittelalterliche Studien*. Stuttgart: Hiersemann, 1966, pp. 74–87.

———. "Die Kölner Nonnenhandschriften und das Skriptorium von

Chelles." *Mittelalterliche Studien*. Stuttgart: Hiersemann, 1966, pp. 16–33.

Bower, Calvin M. *The Principles of Music: An Introduction, Translation, and Commentary*. Dissertation, George Peabody College for Teachers, 1967.

Burgess, Henry E. "Hroswitha and Terence: A Study in Literary Imitation." *Pacific Northwest Conference on Foreign Languages* (1968): 23–29.

Burnes, N.T., and C.J. Reagan. *Concepts of the Hero in the Middle Ages and the Renaissance*. Albany: State University of New York Press, 1975.

Butler, Marguerite. *Hrotsvitha: The Theatrically of her Plays*. New York: Philosophical Library, 1976.

Chamberlain, David. "Musical Learning and Dramatic Action in Hrotsvit's *Pafnutius*." *Studies in Philology* 77:4 (1980): 319–43.

Chambers, E.K. *The Medieval Stage*. Oxford: Clarendon Press, 1903.

Coffman, George R. "A New Approach to Medieval Latin Drama." *Modern Philology* 22 (1925): 239–71.

DeRooter, Florence E. "The Scriptorium." *The Medieval Library*. Ed. James W. Thompson. Chicago: University of Chicago Press, 1939.

Dolger, Franz. "Die Ottonenkaiser und Byzanz." *Karolingische und Ottonische Kunst*. Ed. H. Subin *et al.* Wiesbaden: Franz Steiner, 1957, pp. 49–59.

Dorn, Erhard. *Der sündige Heilige in der Legende des Mittelalters*. Munich: Fink, 1967.

Dorn, Maximilian. *De veteribus grammaticis artis Terentia iudicibus*. Halle: Wischan & Burkhardt, 1806.

Dronke, Peter. *Poetic Individuality in the Middle Ages*. Oxford: Clarendon Press, 1970.

———. *Women Writers of the Middle Ages*. Cambridge: Cambridge Univeristy Press, 1984.

Duckett, Eleanor S. *Death and Life in the Tenth Century*. Ann Arbor: University of Michigan Press, 1967.

Duchting, R. "Hrotsvitha von Gandersheim, Adam Wernher von Themar und Guarino Veronese." *Ruperto Carola* 33 (1963): 77–89.

Dunn, Catherine. *et al. The Medieval Drama and its Claudian Revival*. Washington: Catholic University Press, 1970.

Eis, Gerhard. *Die Quellen des Märtenbuches*. Reichenberg: Sudetendeutscher Verlag, 1932.

Euringer, Sebastian. "Drei Beiträge zur Roswitha Forschung." *Historisches Jahrbuch der Goerres-Gesellschaft zur Pflege der Wissenschaft im Katholischen Deutschland* 54 (1934): 75–83.

Frenken, Goswin. "Eine neue Hrotsvithandschrift." *Gesellschaft für ältere deutsche Geschichtskunde* 44 (1922): 75–83.

Friedlein, G, ed. *Anicii Manlii Torquati Severini Boetii de Institutione Arithmetica Libri Duo*. Leipzig: Minerva, 1966.

Godecki, L., J. Taralon, E. Mätherick and F. Wormland. *Die Zeit der Ottonen and Salier*. Munich: H.C. Beck, 1973.

Grashof, Otto. "Das Benediktinerinnenstift Gandersheim und Hrotsvitha, die 'Zierde der Benediktinerordens.' " *Studien und Mitteilungen aus dem Benediktiner und Cistercienser Orden* 6 (1885): 303–22; 7 (1886): 87–109; 393–404.

Graus, Frantisek. *Volk, Herrscher und Heiliger im Reich der Merovinger.* Prague: Akademie, 1932.

Hagendahl, H. *Augustine and the Latin Classics.* Studia Graeca et Latina Gothoburgensis, 21. Göteborg: Flanders Altiebolag, 1967.

Haight, Anne Lyon. *Hrotsvitha of Gandersheim: Her Life, Times, and Works, and a Comprehensive Bibliography.* New York: Hroswitha Club, 1965.

Haraszti, Zoltan. "The Works of Hrotsvitha." *More Books* 20 (1945): 37–119; 139–73.

Hardison, O.B. *Christian Rite and Christain Drama in the Middle Ages.* Baltimore: Johns Hopkins, 1965.

Homeyer, Helena. " 'Imitatio' und 'Aemulatio' im Werk der Hrotsvitha von Gandersheim." *Studi Medievali* 10 (1968): 966–79.

Hozeski, Bruce. "The Parallel Patterns in Hrotsvitha of Gandersheim, a Tenth Century German Playwright, and in Hildegard of Bingen, a Twelfth Century German Playwright." *Annuale Medievalia* 18 (1977): 42–53.

Hughes, Eril Barnett. "Hrotswitha's Relationship with Terence." Fall, 1982. Southeastern Medieval Association conference. Typescript.

Jackson, W.T.H. *Medieval Literature.* New York, London: Macmillan, 1967.

Jarcho, Boris. "Stilquellen der Hrotsvitha." *Zeitschrift für deutsches Alertum und deutsche literatur* 62 (1925): 236–40.

———. "Zu Hrotsvitha's Wirkungskreis." *Speculum* 2 (1927): 343–44.

Jones, Leslie W., and C.R. Morey. *The Miniatures of the Manuscripts of Terence Prior to the Thirteenth Century.* Princeton: Princeton University Press; London: Oxford University Press, 1978.

Katona, Lajos. "Die altungarische Übersetzung des *Dulcitius* der Hrotswitha." *Allgemeine Zeitung*, Appendix 123 (1900): 6–7.

———. *Irodalmi Tamulmanyai.* 2 vols. Budapest: Kisfaludi Társaság, 1912.

Köpke, Rudolf A. *Hrotsvit von Gandersheim.* Berlin: Ernst S. Mittler und Sohn, 1869.

———. *Die älteste deutsche Dichterin.* Berlin: Ernst S. Mittler und Sohn, 1869.

Kluge, Otto. "Die neulateinische Kunstprosa." *Glotta* 23 (1935): 18–80.

Kronenberg, Kurt. *Roswitha von Gandersheim: Leben und Werk.* Bad Gandersheim: Hertel, 1962.

Kuehne, Oswald. "A Study of the Thais Legend with Special Reference to Hrotsvitha's *Pafnutius.*" Dissertation, University of Pennsylvania, 1922.

Kuhn, Hugo. "Hrotsvit von Gandersheim dichterisches Programm." *Deutsche Vierteljahrschrift* 24 (1950): 181–96.

Langosch, Karl. *Lateinisches Mittelalter: Einleitung in Sprache und Literatur.* Darmstadt: Wissenschaftliche Buchgesellschaft, 1963.

———. *Mittellateinische Dichtung.* Darmstadt: Wissenschaftliche Buchgesellschaft, 1969.

————. *Profile des lateinischen Mittelalters*. Darmstadt: Wissenschaftliche Buchgesellschaft, 1965.

Lefevre, Eckard. *Die Expositionstechnik in den Komödien des Terenz*. Darmstadt: Wissenschaftliche Buchgesellschaft, 1969.

Leyser, K.J. *Rule and Conflict in an Early Medieval Society, Ottonian Saxony*. Bloomington, London: Indiana University Press, 1979.

Lietzmann, D. Hans. "Das Sacramentarium Gregorianum," *Literaturgeschichtliche, geschichtliche Quellen und Forschungen*. Vol. 3, 1921.

Loomis, Roger S., and Gustave Cohen. "Were there Theatres in the Twelfth and Thirteenth Centuries?" *Speculum* 20–21 (1945–46): 92–98.

Lopez, Robert S. *The Tenth Century: Source Problems in World Civilization*. New York, Chicago: Holt, Reinhard and Winston, 1959.

Luca, Kenneth de. "Hrotsvit's 'Imitation' of Terence." *Classical Folia* 28 (1974): 89–102.

Magoulias, Harry J. *Byzantine Christianity: Emperor, Church and the West*. Detroit: Wayne State University Press, 1982.

McGee, Timothy. "The Liturgical Placement of the *Quem Queritis Dialogue*." *Journal of the American Musicological Society* 29 (1976): 1–29.

Menhardt, Hermann. "Eine unbekannte Hrotsvitha-Handschrift." *Zeitschrift für deutsches Altertum und deutsche Literatur* 62 (1925): 233–36.

Murphy, James. *Rhetoric in the Middle Ages*. Berkeley: University of California Press, 1974.

Nagel, Bert. *Hrotsvit von Gandersheim*. Stuttgart: Metzlersche Verlagsbuchhandlung, 1965.

————. "Roswitha von Gandersheim." Appendix to *Ruperto Carola* 33 (1963): 1–40.

Neumann, Friedrich. "Der Denkstil Hrotsvits von Gandersheim." *Festschrift für Hermann Heimpel*. Göttingen: Vandenhoeck und Duprecht, 3 (1972), pp. 37–60.

Newman, Eva M. "The Latinity of the Works of Hrotsvit of Gandersheim." Dissertation, University of Chicago, 1939.

Pavia, Mario N. "Hrotsvitha of Gandersheim." *Folio: Studies in the Christian Perpetuation of the Classics* 3 (1948): 41–45.

Polheim, Karl. *Die lateinische Reimprosa*. Berlin: Weidmann, 1925.

Preminger, A., O.B. Hardison, Jr., and K. Kerrane, eds. *Classical and Medieval Literary Criticism*. New York: Ungar, 1974.

Rand, E.K. "Early Medieval Commentaries on Terence." *Classical Philology* 4 (1909): 359–89.

Reich, Hermann. *Der Mimus*. Berlin: Weidmann, 1903.

Reubelt, Frances. "Hrotsvit and Terence." Dissertation, University of Chicago, 1909.

Reynolds, L.D., and W.G. Wilson. *Scribes and Scholars: A Guide to the Transmission of Greek and Latin Literature*. Oxford: Clarendon Press, 1968.

Rigobon, Marcella. *Il Teatro e la Latinità di Hrotsvitha*. Florence: Olschki, 1930.

Roberts, Arthur J. "Did Hrotsvitha Imitate Terence?" *Modern Language Notes* 16 (1901), cols. 478–82.

Schmidt, Margot. "Orientalischer Einfluss auf die deutsche Literatur: Quellengeschichtliche Studie zu *Abraham* der Hrotsvitha von Gandersheim." *Colloquia Germanica* 2 (1968): 152–87.

Spitz, L. *Conrad: Celtis the German Archhumanist.* Cambridge: Harvard University, 1957.

Sprague, Rosemary. "Hroswitha: Tenth Century Margaret Webster." *Theatre Annual* 13 (1955): 16–31.

Stammler, Wolfgang. *Kleine Schriften zur Literaturgeschichte des Mittelalters.* Bielefeld: Schmidt, 1953.

Sticca, Sandro. "Hrotswitha's *Dulcitius* and Christian Symbolism." *Mediaevel Studies* 32 (1970): 108–27.

———. *The Latin Passion Play: The Origins and Development.* Albany: State Univeristy of New York, 1970.

———. "Hrotsvitha's *Abraham* and Exegetical Tradition." *Acta Conventus Neo-Latini Lovanensis.* Leuven: Leuven University Press, 1973, pp. 633–38.

———. "Metamorphosis of Medieval into Modern." *Translation Spectrum: Essays in Theory and Practice.* Ed. Marilyn G. Rose. Albany: State University of New York, 1981.

Sturm, A. "Das Quadrivium in den Dichtungen Roswithas von Gandersheim." *Studien und Mitteilungen zur Geschichte des Benediktinerordens und seiner Zweige* 38 (1912): 332–38.

Taylor, Henry Osborn. *The Classical Heritage of the Middle Ages.* New York: Harper and Row, 1958.

Thompson, James Westfall. *The Medieval Library.* Chicago: Chicago University Press, 1939.

Vey, Rudolf. *Christliches Theater im Mittelalter und Neuzeit.* Aschaffenburg: P. Pattlock, 1960.

Walther, Hans. *Hrotsvit von Gandersheim.* Bielefeld: Von Velhagen & Klating, 1931.

Wemple, Suzanne F. *Women in Frankish Society.* Philadelphia: University of Pennsylavania, 1981.

Wessner, P., ed. *Donatus: Commentum Terenti.* Bibliotheca Scriptorum Graecorum et Romanorum Teubneriana, vol. 1. Stuttgart: Teubner, 1962.

Weston, Karl E. "The Illustrated Terence Manuscripts." *Harvard Studies in Classical Philology* 14 (1903): 37–54.

Wilson, Katharina. "Hrotsvit and *The Artes*." *Creativity, Influence and Imagination: The World of Medieval Women.* Ed. Constance Berman, Charles Connell and Judith Rothschild. Morgantown: University of West Virginia Press, 1985, pp. 3–14.

———. "Hrotsvit and the Tube: Kennedy Toole and the Problem of Bad TV Programming." *Germanic Notes* 14:4 (1984): 4–5.

———. "Hrotsvit and the Sounds of Harmony and Discord." *Germanic Notes* 14:1 (1983): 54–56.

————. "The Old Hungarian Translation of Hrotsvit's *Dulcitius*: History and Analysis." *Tulsa Studies in Women's Literature* 1:2 (1982): 177–87.

————. "Hrotsvit's *Abraham*: A Lesson in Etymology." *Germanic Notes* 16:1 (1985): 2–4.

————. "Antonomaisa as a Means of Character Definition in the Works of Hrotsvit of Gandersheim." *Rhetorica* 2:1 (1984): 45–53.

————. "*Figmenta* versus *Veritas*." *Tulsa Studies in Women's Literature* 4:1 (1985): 17–33.

————. *Hrotsvit of Gandersheim: "Rara Avis in Saxonia"?* Ann Arbor: Michigan Medieval and Renaissance Monograph Series, 1987.

————. *The Ethics of Authorial Stance: Hrotsvit and her Poetics.* Davis Medieval Texts and Studies. Leiden: Brill, 1988.

Winterfeld, Paul von. *Deutsche Dichter des lateinischen Mittelalters*. Munich: C.H. Beck, 1922.

Young, Karl A. "Homage to Roswitha." *Humanities Association of Canada* 29 (1978): 79–82.

Zeydel, Edwin. "The Authenticity of Hrotsvitha's Works." *Modern Language Notes* 69 (1946): 50–55.

————. "A Chronological Hrotsvitha Bibliography through 1700, with Annotations." *Journal of English and Germanic Philology* 46 (1947): 290–94.

————. " 'Ego Clamor Validus' – Hrotsvitha." *Modern Language Notes* April 64 (1946): 281–83.

————. "Ekkehard's Influence upon Hrotsvitha's Works." *Modern Language Quarterly*, 6 (1943): 333–39.

————. "Knowledge of Hrotsvitha's Works Prior to 1500." *Modern Language Notes* 62 (1944): 382–85.

————. "A Note on Hrotsvit's Aversion to Synalepha." *Philological Quarterly* 23 (1944): 379–81.

————. "On the Two Minor Poems in the Hrotsvitha Codex." *Modern Language Notes* 60 (1945): 373–76.

————. "The Reception of Hrotsvitha by the German Humanists after 1493." *Journal of English and Germanic Philology* 44 (1945): 443–56.

————. "Were Hrotsvitha's Dramas Performed during her Lifetime?" *Speculum* 20 (1943): 443–56.

Index

Compiled by Clayton Foggin